T0318405

Tales of the Crusaders – Remembering the Crusades in Britain

Engaging the Crusades is a series of volumes that offer windows into a newly emerging field of historical study: the memory and legacy of the crusades. Together these volumes examine the reasons behind the enduring resonance of the crusades and present the memory of crusading in the modern period as a productive, exciting, and much needed area of investigation.

Crusading was a part of the rich tapestry of family history, with tales of crusading developed as evidence of heroic endeavour to enhance family prestige. Lists of crusaders were published to satisfy this market and heraldry was a visible means of displaying such lineage. Drawing on extensive research and previously untapped sources, this book charts continuing British interest in the crusades, focusing on the nineteenth century. The volume discusses what was available to read on the subject and how this was discussed in numerous journals. Set in the British context of growing local and regional interest in history and archaeology, the study also considers the physical artefacts associated with the crusades.

Tales of the Crusaders – Remembering the Crusades in Britain is the ideal resource for students and scholars of the history of memory and crusades history in a British context.

Elizabeth Siberry is the author of *The New Crusaders* (2000) and a range of articles about the way in which the crusades and crusaders have been remembered, particularly in nineteenth- and early-twentieth-century Britain.

ENGAGING THE CRUSADES

THE MEMORY AND LEGACY OF THE CRUSADES

SERIES EDITORS

JONATHAN PHILLIPS & MIKE HORSWELL

Engaging the Crusades
The Memory and Legacy of Crusading

Engaging the Crusades is a series of volumes that offer initial windows into the ways in which the crusades have been used in the last two centuries, demonstrating that the memory of the crusades is an important and emerging subject. Together, these studies suggest that the memory of the crusades, in the modern period, is a productive, exciting, and much needed area of investigation.

Series Editors: Jonathan Phillips and Mike Horswell, Royal Holloway, University of London, UK.

In this series:

For more information about this series, please visit:
www.routledge.com/Engaging-the-Crusades/book-series/ETC

Tales of the Crusaders – Remembering the Crusades in Britain

Engaging the Crusades, Volume Six

Elizabeth Siberry

Routledge
Taylor & Francis Group

LONDON AND NEW YORK

First published 2021
by Routledge
2 Park Square, Milton Park, Abingdon, Oxon OX14 4RN

and by Routledge
605 Third Avenue, New York, NY 10017

Routledge is an imprint of the Taylor & Francis Group, an informa business

British Library Cataloguing-in-Publication Data
A catalogue record for this book is available from the British Library

Library of Congress Cataloging-in-Publication Data
Names: Siberry, Elizabeth, author.
Title: Tales of the Crusaders: remembering the
Crusades in Britain / Elizabeth Siberry.
Other titles: Remembering the Crusades in Britain
Description: Abingdon, Oxon; New York, NY: Routledge, [2021] |
Series: Engaging the Crusades; 6 |
Includes bibliographical references and index.
Identifiers: LCCN 2020049612 | ISBN 9780367265243 (hardback) |
ISBN 9780429293641 (ebook)
Subjects: LCSH: Crusades–Historiography. | Crusades in literature. |
Medievalism–Great Britain–History–19th century. |
Memory–Social aspects–Great Britain.
Classification: LCC D156.58 .S535 2021 | DDC 909.07–dc23
LC record available at https://lccn.loc.gov/2020049612

ISBN 13: 978-0-367-26524-3 (hbk)
ISBN 13: 978-0-367-75500-3 (pbk)

Typeset in Times New Roman
by Newgen Publishing UK

Contents

Figures

Acknowledgements

In the course of researching and writing this book, I have incurred many debts of gratitude. Mike Horswell and Adam Knobler have been very generous with their time in reading and commenting on draft chapters and I have also benefitted from informal discussions with them in the margins of conferences and in exchanges of emails, as well, of course, as reading and re-reading their important publications. Kathryn Hurlock has also been very helpful, drawing on her extensive knowledge of crusading and crusaders. And I continue to benefit, even four years after his death, from the wisdom and support shown to me by Professor Jonathan Riley-Smith, who was not only my research supervisor but also a great supporter of my subsequent crusading endeavours.

The final stages of writing this book took place under the strange circumstances of the COVID-19 lockdown and in the aftermath of Storm Dennis, which flooded my house in Wales and necessitated the transport of many boxes of books and notes to an alternative study in London. I have therefore relied greatly on email exchanges with individuals, following up queries on various subjects, from crusading pageants to crossed-legs effigies in parish churches throughout the country. All have been most patient with my questions and added significantly to my knowledge and understanding.

I have also been grateful for the help of library staff, particularly in the London Library, which operated a postal service at the height of lockdown and reopened in early July. Specific thanks are noted in the text and footnotes.

Introduction

In 1825, Sir Walter Scott published *Tales of the Crusaders*, two historical novels titled *The Betrothed* and *The Talisman*. Both are set at the time of the Third Crusade and they were always conceived as a pair looking at the impact of crusading from different angles – the former telling the story of Eveline Berenger, betrothed to the absent crusader Hugh de Lacy, and the latter the adventures of the Scottish crusading knight, Sir Kenneth, later identified as David, Earl of Huntingdon.[1] *The Talisman* is now much better known than *The Betrothed*, not least because of the encounters between King Richard I, known as Richard the Lionheart, and his adversary Saladin.[2] Both books and Scott's other novel set against the background of the Third Crusade, *Ivanhoe*, have however played an important part in shaping the way in which the crusades have been remembered in Britain.

In the Introduction to the 1832 edition, Scott recognized both the popularity of the subject and the challenges it posed for an author:

> He saw plainly enough the interest which might be excited by the very name of the Crusades; but he was conscious, at the same time, that the interest was of a character which it might be more easy to create than to satisfy, and that by the mention of so magnificent a subject each reader might be induced to call up to his imagination a sketch so extensive and so grand that it might not be in the power of the Author to fill it up.[3]

Setting his novels in a broader context, he also quoted examples of crusade stories published and circulating in Europe that illustrate the popularity of and interest in the subject. Scott's novels were widely dramatized and inspired other writers and artists in Britain and elsewhere. Both narrative and pictorial representations have been important in creating memories of key events of the crusades and crusaders.[4]

Borrowing Scott's title, this book will look at the way in which the crusades – and the Third Crusade in particular – because of the accretion of stories that have developed around Richard the Lionheart as a crusading hero, have become part of the collective British national memory. Its focus will be the nineteenth century, when a combination of events in the East (including the Crimean War, the massacre of Bulgarian Christians in 1876, and the Greco–Turkish War of 1897); a nostalgia for the romanticized medieval past; a fascination with chivalry and matters knightly[5]; pride in historical, national, and family achievements; and the greater availability of popular and scholarly history and literature stimulated interest in and debate about the crusading movement. In his book, *The Rise and Fall of British Crusader Medievalism*, published in 2018, Mike Horswell wrote: 'Crusader medievalism – the use and memory of the crusades and crusading rhetoric and imagery in the modern period – was prevalent in nineteenth-century Britain and enjoyed a mutually reinforcing relationship with key strands of British culture'.[6]

The result is a rich tapestry of stories and images that have become part of family, local, regional, and national history and identity. It can sometimes now be difficult to unpack what is fact and what is fiction. The accuracy of a story is, however, not the sole consideration when it comes to the strength and longevity of such tales of courage and noble Christian service. The stories of some individuals and events have inevitably grown with the telling, and the way in which this has happened sheds its own light on interest in and understanding of the crusades. Perceived fact in turn inspired fiction and, in some cases, satire, which in itself is an indicator of popularity and interest. Britain is also rich in physical reminders of the crusades, not least the crossed-legs effigies in many churches, and the nineteenth century witnessed a number of other archaeological discoveries linked (or said to be linked) with the crusades.[7]

Background

In 2000, I published *The New Crusaders: Images of the Crusades in the Nineteenth and Early Twentieth Centuries*, building on a chapter that had appeared in the *Oxford Illustrated History of the Crusades* in 1995.[8] This considered the numerous and varied ways in which the crusades and crusaders were depicted, described, and discussed in nineteenth- and early-twentieth-century Britain: from art to music and literature, against the background of contemporary events and issues.

At the time, this was rather a 'niche' subject in crusade studies, but it is now commonplace for histories of the crusades to take the story up to the present day.[9] My former research supervisor, Jonathan Riley-Smith, to whom I owe a great debt of gratitude for his encouragement and support when I first began to explore this area of research, underlined this continuity of interest in the crusades and crusading in *The Crusades: A History*, first published in 1995 but with several updated editions since, and, of course, his book *The Crusades, Christianity and Islam*, published in 2008.[10]

In several pathfinding articles, Adam Knobler has shown the portability and flexibility of the language and practice of crusading worldwide,[11] and Horswell has shed new light on the memory and legacy of the crusades in Britain between c. 1825 and 1945. All those working in this field have cause to be grateful to him and to Jonathan Phillips, as well of course as the publisher, Routledge,[12] for establishing and championing the *Engaging the Crusades* series. The volumes already published[13] show the international interest in the memory of the crusades and the diversity of research underway.

The crusades remain a subject of considerable interest and controversy in the twenty-first century. Kristin Skottki has written about the challenges posed by the way in which the crusading past has been recreated in the present,[14] and Andrew Elliott has analysed contemporary references to the crusades in mass media for political and other purposes.[15] There remains, however, a rich vein of sources and issues still to be explored and discussed reflecting different aspects of crusade memory and the variety of views expressed.

Continuity and context

Interest in the history of the crusades and efforts to shape how they have been remembered can be traced to the immediate aftermath of the First Crusade. In their study of crusade memory, Megan Cassidy-Welch and Anne Lester wrote: 'Very soon after the first crusaders reached Jerusalem in 1099, perceptions, narratives and indeed memories of those events began to affect and even transform [...] the framework of collective memory'.[16] Those who had participated in the crusades were keen to memorialize their own experiences, and their descendants were similarly interested in celebrating the noble exploits of their ancestors. The research of Nicholas Paul and others has provided a wealth of examples showing the ways in which the crusades have been remembered by such families and communities,[17] and a recent article by James Doherty on the Furnival family underlines the ways in which tales of crusaders were already being adapted in the late Middle Ages.[18]

Medieval English monarchs were acutely aware that the achievements of their crusading forbears reflected glory on their own reigns and actions. Thus, King Henry III celebrated the crusade of his uncle, Richard the Lionheart, in his palaces at Clarendon near Oxford, Winchester, the Tower of London, and Nottingham,[19] and Edward III is said to have inherited a helmet that had belonged to Saladin.[20] Court tournaments re-enacted the legendary encounter between Richard and Saladin, with combatants costumed appropriately,[21] and such images could also be found on tiles in, for example, Chertsey and Neath Abbeys. Edward III's son, the Black Prince, like a number of contemporaries, possessed a tapestry of a military encounter between Richard and Saladin and this was depicted on other decorative artefacts, such as carved ivory caskets.[22]

Richard's crusading exploits also inspired a number of literary romances, and the work of Lee Manion has underlined the wealth of material on this subject in medieval and early modern literature, which was made more accessible through the advent of printing.[23]

This combination of literary tradition and crusade memory, coupled with the ongoing threat to Europe from the Turkish Ottoman Empire, meant, as Norman Housley noted in his history of the later crusades, 'the crusade was carried into the sixteenth century as a factor in people's lives'.[24]

I have written elsewhere[25] about the influence of Torquato Tasso's poem *Gerusalemme Liberata*, published in 1581, ten years after the naval victory at Lepanto and set against the background of the First Crusade. Books, poems, and plays about the crusades continued to be written and performed in the sixteenth and seventeenth centuries, and scenes of crusade battles and individual leaders were depicted in paintings, tapestries, and opera. Tudor and Stuart gentry families were keen to claim a crusading ancestor and, as will be seen later, were not shy of creating one if the appropriate evidence was not readily available. This was also the period when copies were made of medieval rolls of arms, and when Sir Edmund Knightley of Fawsley Hall, Northamptonshire, built his Great Hall in 1537, he chose the coats of arms of the family, Richard the Lionheart, and 26 knights who had accompanied him on his crusade to decorate its grand fireplace.[26] Godfrey of Bouillon was also one of the Nine Worthies to be seen on the façade of Montacute House in Somerset and the painted ceiling of Crathes Castle in Perthshire, both of which date from this era.[27]

The first full analysis in English of the causes and events of the crusades was Thomas Fuller's popular *The History of the Holy Warre*, published in 1639, which ran to several editions.[28] Other histories and collections of sources, such as Jacques Bongars's *Gesta Dei per Francos* (Hanover, 1611) and Louis Maimbourg's *Histoire des croisades pour la deliverance de la Terre Sainte* (1675–6), appeared in the seventeenth century, and the range of crusade texts and historiography grew at pace in subsequent centuries.[29]

Against this background, it was no accident that the composer George Frederick Handel chose Richard the Lionheart as the subject of his opera *Riccardo Primo*, which opened the season at the Haymarket Theatre in London in November 1727, and the dedicatory sonnet by the Italian librettist Paolo Rolli drew an explicit link between the new King George II and Richard:

> The Royal stage presents to you your warrior predecessor [...]. But if, O great king, you desire more from the living hero so powerfully portrayed, turn your noble mind to your own ideas [...], say that you have in your hand not only the destinies of the East but, like Jove, those of the whole world.[30]

The dramatic appeal of encounters between Christian and 'Saracen' was not just a matter for royal entertainment. In 1809, the *Cabinet Cyclopaedia* recorded a curious drama, witnessed on the borders of Lancashire and Yorkshire, on Good Friday:

> Saracens and Christians, Saladin, Richard, Edward and other notable personages [were] represented by some young men, whose uncouth fantastic garbs were not the least remarkable feature of the scene. After a long dialogue, in verse, the language of which, though somewhat modernized, was evidently of considerable antiquity, the Soldan and Lionheart crossed their tin swords until the former was sent 'howling to his native hell'.[31]

This reference comes in a chapter on the early history of the English stage and there is no further sourcing or indication that this was a more common occurrence. It does, however, suggest that traditions of crusading survived in popular culture many years after the actual events.

Figures from the crusades were regarded as exemplars, and when General Sir Redvers Buller VC died in 1908, his family commissioned the influential church architect William Caroe to design an elaborate stone reredos as a memorial in the parish church of Crediton, in Devon. This included a figure of Godfrey of Bouillon (Figure 0.1), paired with the prophet Joshua, which probably symbolized their successful

Figure 0.1 Godfrey de Bouillon from the Buller Memorial at Crediton
      Parish Church
Source: Courtesy of Crediton Parish Church.

sieges of Jerusalem and Jericho, respectively, and Buller's own relief of
Ladysmith in 1900, during the second Boer war.[32] And at the Strawberry
Hill Gothic-style Eridge Castle in Kent, the Marquess of Abergavenny
commissioned the artist Thomas Willement to produce designs for a
frieze of crusader knights, perhaps in recognition of his Nevill crusade
ancestors.[33]

Private theatricals were popular in many families including royalty,
and one tableau at Osborne House in 1894, almost certainly inspired by
The Talisman,[34] featured Queen Victoria's sons-in-law, the Marquis of
Lorne and Prince Henry of Battenberg, as Richard the Lionheart and
Saladin.[35] There is also other evidence of events that occurred during
the crusades, featuring in historical pageants in different towns and
regions of Britain, celebrating local history and figures.[36]

There have been a number of studies of the way in which the history
of the crusades, and the Third Crusade in particular, was evoked during
and in memory of the First World War,[37] and the Oxford Pageant of

Victory in 1919 included a scene showing Richard I returning from his crusade and hearing a prediction given by a monk of the recapture of Jerusalem some 700 years later:

> Unto your majesty it is not given to hold that same land of Palestine [...]. Many moons shall wax and wane, many seasons change, and centuries roll by, ere Christian hands shall once more raise the cross above Jerusalem. But this shall be in seven hundred years from now, in a great Crusade, the mightiest the world has ever known. Hard shall be the fight and long, but the Lord shall give them victory! [...] Quietly, and with all humility shall the conquerors enter Jerusalem, and claim it thus for God and Christ for evermore.[38]

Whilst, as Horswell has shown, there was less use of crusade imagery as the twentieth century progressed, it still played (and plays) a part in the memory of the Second World War. For example, Easton Lodge airfield in Essex was the base for the American 386th Bomb Group, known as The Crusaders, and a memorial stained-glass window in the American chapel at the church in Little Easton, dedicated in October 1990, shows an airman and two crusaders 'with Christian banners expressing the continuity of the fight for Right'.[39] Crusade imagery was also used in the 1945 Empire Day celebration at the Royal Albert Hall in London in which a knight in shining armour knelt before an altar and signalled men and women to rededicate themselves to the service of God and mankind and follow him in the 'Great Crusade against the forces of evil'.[40] As I have already mentioned, current research published in this series underlines the continuity of memory and diversity in more modern late-twentieth and twenty-first-century examples.

Approach to the subject

Memories therefore have built on memories created over previous centuries. Although I will cite some examples from other periods and outside Britain, my focus here will be the nineteenth century. And, whilst I will inevitably refer back to *The New Crusaders*, I will draw on a range of new sources that I believe show an even richer picture of how and why the crusades and crusaders were remembered in Britain in this period.

A first step is to consider what was available to read about the crusades, and Chapter 1 will look at books and articles on the subject and the range of opinions to be found in periodicals, magazines, and newspapers. The latter sources have not previously been considered in any detail and reveal a wide and often well-informed debate on the crusades that was sometimes, but not always, influenced by current events. I will also look at the evidence of what was actually read, from library records, footnotes, and contemporary diaries and letters. Memory is created not only by what we read but also what we see, and Chapter 2 will discuss some of the physical monuments said to relate to the crusade, which could (and still can) be found in churches and historic collections throughout Britain. Moreover, discoveries in archaeology and research into local history in the nineteenth century brought the events and participants of the crusades to much greater local, regional, and national attention. Many such monuments commemorated individuals, and Chapter 3 will consider the interest and enthusiasm in identifying and claiming crusade ancestors. Lists of crusaders were published to satisfy this market, and a sixteenth-century copy of a medieval roll of arms, now in the Bodleian Library in Oxford, which has hitherto received only limited attention from crusade historians, seems to have been a key source for later historians and genealogists. Heraldry was a very visible and colourful way of celebrating family history, therefore, Chapter 4 will examine the ways in which symbols on coats of arms have been associated with participation in the crusades. Linking 'fact' and fiction, the final chapter will look at the variety of legends and stories that have grown up about the fate of the absent or returning crusader and those left behind in Europe. Taken together, these themes will, I hope, provide different and new perspectives on how and why the crusades have become part of the British national collective memory.

Notes

1 The genesis of both novels is discussed in the 2009 Edinburgh editions by John Ellis.
2 For the ways in which the relationship between the two protagonists has inspired writers and artists, see Mike Horswell, 'Saladin and Richard the Lionheart. Entangled Memories' in *The Making of Crusading Heroes and Villains*, eds. Mike Horswell and Kristen Skottki (London, 2020), pp. 75–94.
3 Walter Scott, *Tales of the Crusaders: The Betrothed* (New York, 1825), p. ix.
4 For the influence of Scott's novels, see Siberry, *The New Crusaders* (Aldershot, UK, 2000), pp. 125–9. More generally, see Martin Meisel, *Realizations: Narrative, Pictorial and Theatrical Arts in Nineteenth-Century England* (Princeton, NJ, 1983), p. 3.
5 See in particular Mark Girouard, *The Return to Camelot. Chivalry and the English Gentleman* (New Haven, CT, 1981).
6 Mike Horswell, *The Rise and Fall of British Crusader Medievalism c. 1825–1945* (Abingdon, UK, 2018), p. 3.

7 Astrid Swenson, 'Crusader Heritages and Imperial Preservation', *Past and Present* 226 (2015), Supplement 10, pp. 27–56, has looked at the ways in which the preservation of the physical heritage has been used in a colonial context. See also Pierre Nora, *Realms of Memory: The Construction of the French Past*, 3 vols (New York, 1998).

8 Siberry, *New Crusaders*, and 'Images of the Crusades in the Nineteenth and Twentieth Centuries' in *The Oxford Illustrated History of the Crusades*, ed. Jonathan Riley-Smith (Oxford, 1995), pp. 365–86 (now being updated).

9 For example, Jonathan Phillips, *Holy Warriors. A Modern History of the Crusades* (London, 2009); Mike Horswell, 'New Crusaders and Crusading Echoes: The Modern Memory and Legacy of the Crusades in the West and Beyond' in *The Cambridge History of the Crusades*, ed. Jonathan Phillips (Cambridge, UK, forthcoming); Anthony Bale, ed., *The Cambridge Companion to the Literature of the Crusades* (Cambridge, UK, 2019).

10 Jonathan Riley-Smith, *The Crusades: A History*, 3rd edition (London, 2014), and *The Crusades, Christianity and Islam* (New York, 2008).

11 For example, Adam Knobler, 'Holy Wars, Empires, and the Portability of the Past: The Modern Uses of Medieval Crusades', *Comparative Studies in Society and History* 48 (2006), pp. 293–325.

12 Routledge published a number of works on the crusades in the nineteenth century, so their archives might offer further insights.

13 There are now five volumes in the Engaging the Crusades series: *Perceptions of the Crusades from the Nineteenth to the Twenty-First Century*, eds. Mike Horswell and J. Phillips (2018); *The Crusades in the Modern World*, eds. Mike Horswell and Akil N. Awan (2020); *Controversial Histories – Current Views on the Crusades*, eds. Felix Hinz and Johannes Meyer-Hamme (2020); *The Making of Crusading Heroes and Villains*, eds. Mike Horswell and Kristin Skottki (2020); and *Playing the Crusades*, ed. Robert Houghton (2021).

14 Kristin Skottki, 'The Dead, the Revived and the Recreated Pasts: "Structural Amnesia" in Representations of Crusade History' in *Perceptions of the Crusades from the Nineteenth to the Twenty-First Centuries*, eds. Mike Horswell and Jonathan Phillips (London, 2018), pp. 107–33.

15 Andrew B.R. Elliott, *Medievalism, Politics and Mass Media* (Woodbridge, UK, 2017).

16 Megan Cassidy-Welch and Anne E. Lester, 'Memory and Interpretation: New Approaches to the Study of the Crusades', *Journal of Medieval History* 40 (2014), p. 235.

17 Nicholas L. Paul, *To Follow in their Footsteps. The Crusades and Family Memory in the High Middle Ages* (Ithaca, NY, 2012); Nicholas L. Paul and Suzanne Yeager, *Remembering the Crusades. Myth, Image and Identity* (Baltimore, MD, 2012) and Megan Cassidy-Welch, ed., *Remembering the Crusades and Crusading* (Abingdon, UK, 2017).

18 James Doherty, 'Commemorating the Past in Late Medieval England: The Worksop Priory Tabula', *English Historical Review*, 2020. Emma Mason, 'Legends of the Beauchamps' Ancestors: The Use of Baronial Propaganda in Medieval England', *Journal of Medieval History* 10 (1984), pp. 25–40,

also describes how the crusading history of the Beauchamp family was adapted for propaganda purposes.

19 Laura J. Whatley, 'Romance, Crusade and the Orient in King Henry III's Royal Chambers', *Viator* 44 (2013), pp. 175–99; Christopher Tyerman, *England and the Crusades 1095–1588* (Chicago, 1988), p. 117 n. 26. See also Matthew M. Reeve, 'The Painted Chamber at Westminster, Edward I and the Crusade', *Viator* 37 (2006), pp. 189–221.

20 Timothy Guard, *Chivalry, Kingship and Crusade: The English Experience in the Fourteenth Century* (Woodbridge, UK, 2013), p. 165.

21 See Chapter 4.

22 Juliet Vale, *Edward III and Chivalry: Chivalric Society and its Context 1270–1350* (Woodbridge, UK, 1982), p. 131 n. 153; Roger S. Loomis, 'The Pas Saladin in Art and Heraldry' in *Studies in Art and Literature for Belle da Costa Greene*, ed. Dorothy Miner (Princeton, NJ, 1954), pp. 83–92.

23 Lee Manion, *Narrating the Crusades: Loss and Recovery in Medieval and Early Modern English Literature* (Cambridge, UK, 2014), and 'Renaissance Crusading Literature: Memory, Translation and Adaptation' in *The Cambridge Companion to the Literature of the Crusades*, ed. Anthony P. Bale (Cambridge, UK, 2019), pp. 232–48. See also Tyerman, *England and the Crusades*, pp. 304–5.

24 Norman Housley, *The Later Crusades from Lyons to Alcazar, 1274–1580* (Oxford, 1992), p. 420.

25 Siberry, 'Tasso and the Crusades: History of a Legacy', *Journal of Medieval History* 19 (1993), pp. 163–9. See also Jason Lawrence, *Tasso's Art and Afterlives* (Manchester, 2017).

26 See Deborah Gage, 'A Short History of Fawsley, Northants', *FIRLE*, <https://firle.com/a-short-history-of-fawsley-northamptonshire>, [accessed 20 October 2020].

27 See Bruce Dickens, 'The Nine Unworthies' in *Medieval Literature and Civilization. Studies in Memory of G.N. Garmonsway*, eds. Derek A. Pearsall and Ronald A. Waldron (London, 1969), pp. 228–33.

28 See Bernard Hamilton, 'An Anglican View of the Crusades: Thomas Fuller's *The Historie of the Holy Warre*', *Studies in Church History* 49 (2013), pp. 121–31.

29 For the historiography of the crusades, see Christopher Tyerman, *The Debate on the Crusades* (Manchester, 2011).

30 Alan Yorke-Long, 'George II and Handel', *History Today* (1951), pp. 33–9.

31 Dionysius Lardner, ed., *Cabinet Cyclopaedia, Lives of the Most Eminent Literary and Scientific Men of Great Britain: Early Writers*, vol. 1 (London, 1835), pp. 183–4.

32 Jennifer M. Freeman, *W.D. Caroe: His Architectural Achievement* (Manchester, 1990), pp. 237–41; 'The Buller Memorial', <www.creditonparishchurch.org.uk/history/the-buller-memorial>, [accessed 20 October 2020]. I am grateful to Crediton Parish Church for the image published here.

33 Thomas Willement, *Album of Designs and Illustrations for Presentation to Lord Abergavenny* (1818).

34 Talisman-inspired depictions of Richard and Saladin appeared in many different media, including as elaborate gold and silver table centrepieces for use in formal banquets. See *Illustrated London News,* 3 July 1852, p. 16.

35 Richard Schoch, *Queen Victoria and the Theatre of Her Age* (Manchester, 2004), p. 25. Princess Louise, the Marchioness of Lorne, was a talented sculptor and one of her works was a bronze equestrian figure of Richard the Lionheart on display at the family home, Inveraray Castle, in Scotland. See James Lees-Milne, *Diaries 1942–54: Ancestral Voices and Prophesying Peace* (London, 1975), p. 219.

36 'The Redress of the Past: Historical Pageants in Britain', <www. historicalpageants.ac.uk>, [accessed 20 October 2020]. Pageants featuring scenes from the history of the crusades included the Abinger (Surrey) pageant, written by the author E.M. Forster, with music by Ralph Vaughan Williams; Reading 1920; Portchester, Hampshire, 1932; Boston, Lincolnshire, 1951. See also pp. 92–4. Crusaders also appeared in fancy dress balls and events. See Siberry, *New Crusaders,* pp. 128–30; *Illustrated London News,* 3 October 1843, p. 343; 1 June 1844, p. 348; 17 January 1845, p. 4.

37 Stefan Goebel, *The Great War and Medieval Memory: War, Remembrance and Medievalism in Britain and Germany, 1914–1940* (Cambridge, UK, 2007); Mike Horswell, *British Crusader Medievalism,* pp. 113–37; Siberry, 'Memorials to Crusaders: The Use of Crusade Imagery in First World War Memorials in Britain' in *The Legacy of the Crusades: History and Memory,* eds. Kurt Jensen and Torben Nielsen, vol. 2 (Turnhout, Belgium, forthcoming).

38 'Historical Pageants in Britain, <www.historicalpageants.ac.uk>. Berenice de Bergerac, *The Oxford Pageant of Victory 1919* (Oxford, 1919). Bergerac had also staged *Glorious England: A Tale of the Crusades* at the Sheldonian Theatre in Oxford on 9 January 1918, a month after Allenby's entry into Jerusalem, which told the story of the attempted poisoning of the crusading Edward I.

39 Trevor Allen, 'WWII Martin B-26 Marauder Crews', *B26.com,* <www.b26. com/historian/martin_b26_marauder.htm>, [accessed 20 October 2020]

40 John M. Mackenzie, 'In Touch with the Infinite: The BBC and the Empire, 1923–53' in *Imperialism and Popular Culture* (Manchester, 1986), pp. 175–6.

1 Reading about the crusades

The invention of the printing press in the fifteenth century enabled the publication of sources for the history of the crusades, and by the nineteenth century, facilitated by cheaper paper and developments in printing technology, books on the crusades and editions or translations of sources had become both more easily available and affordable.[1] In addition, access to books was much greater through the various public libraries in cities, towns, and villages throughout Britain. There were also numerous smaller circulating, subscription, and community libraries, as well as the collections of aristocratic houses, gentry, and professionals, such as lawyers and doctors, and we know that some private libraries made their collections available to friends, family, staff, and neighbours.[2]

The aim of this chapter, which uses hitherto untapped sources, is to look at not only at what was available to read, but also examples of individual reading records. In addition, I discuss how works about the crusades were advertised and their content debated in the numerous periodicals, magazines, and newspapers of the day. This provides a much richer picture of the diversity of opinion about the crusades and the different perspectives taken and discussed. In some cases, one can see that interest was sparked by current events and religious affiliations, but in others it stemmed from a more general interest and pride in British history.

A bibliography

At the turn of the nineteenth century, Robert Watt, the son of a farmer from Ayrshire in Scotland, who had studied and practised medicine in Glasgow and Edinburgh, began work on a massive bibliography titled *Bibliotheca Britannica, or a General Index to British and Foreign Literature*, which was intended to list books alphabetically by both author and subject and to serve as 'a universal catalogue of all the authors with which this country is acquainted, whether of its own or of the continent'. Watt died in 1819 before the work was published, but it appeared first in parts between 1819 and 1824 and then in four volumes in 1824. It included a section on the crusades, which shows that some readers at least had access to early editions of crusade sources, such as the collection published by Bongars in 1611; histories by Maimbourg (1675–6) and Voltaire (*Essai*, 1751, and translated as *History of the Crusades*, 1753); and some contemporary poems inspired by the crusades.[3]

Public and private libraries

Whilst Edinburgh and London were major centres of publishing and literary activity, the published catalogues of a diverse range of libraries throughout Britain provide an insight into which books were purchased for their increasing shelves and reveal a range of primary and secondary works on the crusades, including Joseph Francois Michaud's four-volume history (published 1811–22 in French and then from 1852 in an English translation) as well as books by British historians, such as Charles Mills, whose two-volume history of the crusades was published in 1820 and ran to several editions.

The existence of a book does not, of course, provide evidence that it was read, but more research is now being undertaken that looks at surviving borrowing records, which help to answer the question of who borrowed what and when. In this context, the records of three very different libraries – the private subscription London Library in St James's Square, Mayfair; the Bristol Library Society; and the privately funded borrowing library at Innerpeffray in Perthshire in Scotland – offer some interesting insights into reading habits.

The records of the London Library, founded in 1841, show that the Library had a good selection of primary and secondary works on the crusades, and that in the mid-1840s and 1850s, members borrowed Mills, an 1842 history of the Templars by London lawyer Charles Addison, and Michaud, as well as the ubiquitous Tasso and the historical novels of George Payne Rainsford James.[4]

In Bristol, the Bristol Library Society was founded in 1773, with a membership reflecting the diverse nature of the busy trading city,[5] and its catalogues and borrowing records provide additional insight into contemporary reading habits. They show, for example, that Thomas Johnes's translation of Joinville's history of Saint Louis was borrowed regularly in the years following its publication in 1807, as was Mills.[6]

On a different scale, records have also survived of borrowings at Innerpeffray in Perthshire. Founded in 1690 by the Drummond family, Innerpeffray is Scotland's oldest borrowing library. It has only a handful of books relating to the crusades: Fuller's *History of the Holy Warre*, Tasso, and the crusade tales of Walter Scott. Nevertheless, the borrowing entries add another piece to the jigsaw, showing that in 1808, 1812, and 1887, three local residents, including one described as a 'scholar', borrowed Tasso, and in 1859 and 1861, a local farmer and then a pupil at Taylor's Institution (a school founded for the education of the poor children of nearby Crieff) borrowed Fuller's *History*.[7]

The visual image

Many of the books about the crusades were also illustrated, both with black and white engravings and in colour, creating a separate source of image and memory. For example, the 1877 edition of Michaud's *History* included 100 full-page engravings by the prolific French illustrator Gustave Dore (Figure 1.1). These depicted the main events of

Figure 1.1 Gustave Dore, *Godfrey Enters Jerusalem*, 1877
Source: WikiArt, public domain.

the crusades from the First Crusade up to the battle of Lepanto in 1571, and engravings such as 'Troubadours singing the Glories of the Crusades', 'The Departure', and 'The Return' reflect the romanticised way in which artists of the period tended to portray the crusades.[8] Dore's illustrations were also used in a variety of other publications about the crusades.[9] As one historian of Victorian Painting has commented: 'Many famous events were fixed into the national consciousness by painted reconstructions, later reproduced in encyclopaedias and school textbooks, until the images took on lives of their own'.[10]

The crusades also, of course, inspired numerous nineteenth-century artists throughout Europe and North America whose works could be seen in galleries and public exhibitions.[11]

Periodicals

Information about books on the crusades was also widely available in the many periodicals that were published, on a weekly, monthly, or quarterly basis, from the late-eighteenth century onwards, principally in London and Edinburgh, but also in smaller numbers in other major cities. It has been estimated that between 1790 and 1842 over 4,000 periodicals were published in Britain, and this number had increased at least tenfold by the end of the century.[12] Such publications were distributed throughout the country and would also have been sent to eager readers in the British Empire. For example, 15,000 copies of the *Gentleman's Magazine*, which was established in 1731 and based at St John's Gate in Clerkenwell, were printed each month in the 1750s and reached a much wider audience through libraries, inns, and coffee houses. A recent study noted, 'its national circulation bound together readers from the metropolis, provinces and colonies, facilitating a process of debate and information, which flowed in all directions'.[13]

Although authors of articles and reviews were usually anonymous, research has shown that they included key literary and political figures of the day and covered almost every subject of interest, including the crusades. In his *Index to Periodical Literature* published in 1882, William Poole wrote:

> The best writers and the great statesmen of the world, where they formerly wrote a book or pamphlet, now contribute an article to a leading review or magazine, and it is read before the month is ended in every country in Europe [...]. Every question [...] finds its latest and freshest interpretation in the current periodicals.[14]

Essays and reviews

New books were widely advertised, and book reviews might cover not only the specific publication but also the broader subject of the crusades. They often ran to some 10 or more pages and represented a variety of views, according to the perspective of the author and the editorial position of the journal in question, as well as displaying a detailed knowledge of the subject matter and source material.

As has been discussed elsewhere, the crusades were chosen as the subject for international and national essay competitions[15] and a number of essays on the subject of their short and long-term impact and influence can be found in contemporary periodicals. The sense in which the crusades were seen as part of the 'fabric' of British life and memory is reflected in rather florid language in a review published in *The Spectator* in May 1844:

> On almost every interest of man they have indented their history. The gallantry of far later conflicts on the strand of Acre is forgotten in the feats of Coeur de Lion in this cause [...]. The story is told by the cross-bilted sword and the recumbent figures of our monumental effigies. The signs of our common hostelries still show the formidable heads of Saracen and Turk.[16]

Two examples illustrate the range of authors attracted by this subject and the diversity of views.

Sir Archibald Alison

In 1846, the lawyer and historian, Sir Archibald Alison, author of a popular history of Europe, published a 30-page essay titled 'The Crusades' in the conservative Edinburgh-based *Blackwood's Magazine*.[17] Alison's opening sentence declared that 'the crusades are, beyond all question, the most extraordinary and memorable movement that ever took place in the history of mankind' and the motive of those who took part was the 'rescue' of the Holy Sepulchre: 'For this they lived, for this they died. For this, millions of warriors abandoned their native seats, and left their bones to whiten the fields of Asia [...]. No maiden would look at a lover who had not served in Palestine; few could resist those who had'.

Alison described Tasso's *Gerusalemme* as the epic of this heroic age and, recalling Homer's *Iliad*, declared: 'Saladin was a mightier prince than Hector; Godfrey was a nobler character than Agamemnon;

Richard immeasurably more heroic than Achilles'. But he did not consider that poetry had sufficiently captured the real spirit of the crusades.
Turning to history, he criticized the views of writers, such as Voltaire,
described as treating these heroic events with 'flippant persiflage' and
credited those from Britain and elsewhere in Europe who had drawn
attention to the positive impact of the crusades on, for example, arts
and science. For Alison, however, the most important legacy was the
focus on 'generous and disinterested objects':

> The noble and heroic feelings, which have taken such hold of the
> mind of modern Europe and distinguish it from any other age
> of quarter of the globe, have mainly arisen from the profound
> emotions awakened by the mingling of the passions of chivalry
> with the aspirations of devotion during the crusades.

Alison's language is colourful – with a tendency towards the superla-
tive – but he certainly reflected a strand of opinion, and his essay shows
his breadth of reading on the subject. He knew Gibbon and Mills's histories and he cites works by French and Italian historians, with particular praise given to the work of Michaud:

> A historian peculiarly qualified for the great undertaking which he
> has accomplished, of giving a full and accurate, yet graphic history
> of the crusades [...]. Deeply imbued with the romantic and chival-
> rous ideas of the olden time, a devout Catholic as well as a sincere
> Christian, he brought to the annals of the crusaders a profound
> admiration for their heroism, a sincere respect for their disinter-
> estedness, a graphic eye for their delineation, a warm sympathy for
> their devotion.[18]

Hannah Lawrance

In 1853, a rather different essay on the subject appeared in the *British
Quarterly Review*, which has been described as the 'voice of dissent
without dissidence' and was aimed at a middle-class non-conformist
readership.[19] Its author was Hannah Lawrance, a historian and journalist, as well as a lifelong member of the Congregational Church, who
penned a variety of articles on medieval history and literature with a
particular focus on the primary sources.[20] Her article was titled 'The
Crusades as Described by Crusaders' and described the main events of
the crusades. She cited as her key sources Bongars; the edition of the
Itinerarium published as part of a collection of English historians by

Thomas Gale in 1687; an 1824 edition of Geoffrey of Villehardouin's history of the Fourth Crusade; and Johnes's 1807 translation of Joinville.

In an article of nearly 40 pages, Lawrance was eager to highlight the 'crusade spirit', and her concluding paragraph revealed her own religious affiliation:

> So the serried hosts of the Croises [...] kept back, at the cost of their lives, that fierce inundation of eastern barbarism, holding out until the danger that menaced western Europe had passed away, and she was free to pursue her onward career – to fling defiance at St Peter's chair, even as she had flung defiance at the Moslem host, and to become the centre of learning, science, of civilization to the whole world.[21]

Debate and discussion

The essays on the influence of the crusades by Oxford student Frederick Oakeley and the Gottingen Professor Arnold Heeren were often quoted, and one journal, *The British Controversialist and Literary Magazine*, subtitled as established 'for the purpose of forming a suitable medium for the deliberate discussion of important questions in religion, philosophy, history, politics and social economy', encouraged its readers to share and debate positive and negative views of the crusades. In 1852 and 1870, it published two series of exchanges of views titled 'Were the effects of the crusades favourable to the civilization and moral elevation of the people?', and 'Were the crusades beneficial to social progress?'

The authors were anonymous (using just Christian names or initials) but again suggest a wide variety of views on and discussion of the subject. Even allowing for an individual author's desire to display his erudition, they also assume a degree of prior knowledge from personal reading. The question 'Were the crusades beneficial to social progress?', posed in the 1870 volume, prompted six articles – three presenting a negative view and three an affirmative one.[22] They covered issues such as whether the crusades: fostered peace in Europe; encouraged Christians to visit the Holy Land; increased the power of the papacy; and distracted men's minds from the true causes of social improvement. Tasso's romanticized view of crusading was often quoted, along with the familiar histories of Mills, Michaud, and Gibbon. One contributor, signing just as MFA, declared:

> I shall, for brevity's sake, for the present assume that the reader is acquainted with the material facts of the history of the crusades,

as related by Gibbon, chaps 58–61; Hallam in his 'History of the Middle Ages'; Charles Mills's 'History of the crusades'; the translation of Michaud's 'History of the Crusades'; Ockley's 'History of the Saracens'; Heeren's 'Essay on the Influence of the Crusades' or some other work of authority; as it would be impossible, within any reasonable limits, to give even an outline of these endeavours [...]. Our object is not historical, but critical; we do not require to describe, but to discuss.[23]

MFA also noted the way in which the term crusade was now used to denote a variety of social and other campaigns.

In 1868, the editor of the *British Controversialist* also published *The Debater's Handbook of Controversial Topics*. The list of over a thousand subjects included the topic chosen by the journal for 1852, and another – 'Which supplies the best history of the crusades: Heeren, Mills, Michaud or Wilken?' – which again indicates an expectation of some prior knowledge and study.[24]

There were a number of debating societies in London and other major cities that seem to have catered to all ages, and according to one contributor to the *British Controversialist*, the crusades were:

one of the most commonplace of those subjects on which members of discussion clubs engage on the hot contest of wordy conflict. Though a commonplace topic, it is not an unimportant one, and we hope that it may be treated in such a manner in these pages as may show those who do battle thereafter on this topic how to apply thought as well as research to the consideration of those questions which have appeared upon debaters' programmes with almost wearisome frequency and iteration.[25]

An intriguing comment in the journal of Lady Knightley of Fawsley for 6 May 1887 suggests that such debates were quite popular:

Late in the afternoon to a meeting of the Girl's Fortnightly Debating Society [...] presided over by Lord Wolseley and most amusing it was. The subject was the Crusades, did they do most good or harm to Europe? And it was duly debated and discussed [...] all voted that the good predominated but what struck me with amazement was that among 8 or 9 girls under 21 not one was found to speak with enthusiasm of the high and noble ideas which underlay the Crusades at first, whatever they may eventually have degenerated into. The whole movement was characterized as fanaticism, every sort of utilitarian argument for and against was brought forward and it was left to Lord Wolseley, the grey headed soldier, to decide upon that most important point, which he did with considerable emphasis.[26]

By their very nature, records of such discussions may be rare, but newspapers did on occasion publish summaries of public lectures on the subject. For example, in 1897, against the background of the Greco–Turkish War, the Headmaster of Gowerton School, near Swansea in Wales, gave a lecture titled 'The Crusades: Their Causes, Course and Effects' at the local Free Library, which was reported in the local newspaper.[27]

The range of views on the subject is further illustrated by the publications of William Stewart Ross, the Scottish-born editor of the *Secular Review*, a weekly journal of agnosticism, and for a time Secretary of the Lambeth Radical Association, who styled himself Saladin. He produced a number of articles and pamphlets about the crusades from a secularist perspective in the 1880s, concluding that they represented:

> The maddest and bloodiest picture in the history of the world [...] everywhere hideous with swords and skeletons and cinders. Like everything else in Christian history, such a refulgent halo of sanctity and romance has been flung over it as to render its true and horrible lineaments almost imperceptible [...]. Say what you may about the opening up of commerce and the introduction of oriental culture, every footprint of the crusades is marked with blood, every step is profaned with lust, every impulse is tainted with madness.

Ross argued that Saladin was the 'only glorious name connected with the crusades'.[28] Curiously he was also the author of *Lays of Romance and Chivalry*, which included a poem about Richard the Lionheart at Ascalon.[29]

Articles on the crusades

The lively correspondence on archaeological discoveries relating to the crusades is discussed in the next chapter, but periodicals also included articles on other aspects of crusade history. Thus in 1804, *Archaeologia* published a 'Memoir on the Vicissitudes of the Principality of Antioch During the Crusades',[30] and the weekly *Saturday Review of Politics, Literature, Science and Art* printed articles on the Conquest of Lisbon; the Financing of the crusades; Joinville and Saint Louis; Saladin in

Cairo; and the use of the term crusade in relation to contemporary campaigns and wars, as well as reviews of books on the subject.[31]

Authors of monographs on the crusades also published articles. For example, the soldier, explorer, and antiquarian Charles Conder, whose history of the Latin Kingdom of Jerusalem was published by the Palestine Exploration Fund in 1897, wrote an article for *Blackwood's Magazine* in the same year, titled 'Saladin and Richard: The Eastern Question in the Twelfth Century', again against the background of the Greco–Turkish War. He also reviewed Reinhold Rohricht's *Regesta Regni Hierosolymitana* and Ernest Rey's *Les Colonies Franques en Syrie* for the *Edinburgh Review* in 1894. His review was subtitled 'The Results of the Crusades' and provided a platform for a broader exposition of the impact of the crusades.[32]

Records of reading

There are other sources for reading habits in this period. Some readers, such as Gladstone, recorded in detail what they read and with marginal annotations,[33] and the letters, diaries, and autobiographies of other prominent figures give another perspective on attitudes to and interest in the crusades.

Three examples illustrate the range of interest and opinions in late-eighteenth- and nineteenth-century Britain – the poet Robert Southey, the designer William Morris, and the lawyer Sir James Mackintosh – as well as the sources of their knowledge on the subject.

Robert Southey

The poet and historian Robert Southey was born in 1774 into a family of Somerset yeoman stock, but wrote that he 'should like to believe that one of my ancestors had served in the crusades'.[34] He was introduced to Tasso's *Gerusalemme* as a child via a circulating library and the copy that he was subsequently given remained one of his most treasured books.[35] He seems to have had a real interest in the history of the crusades, and in the spring of 1795, when he was living in Bristol, he gave a public lecture on 'State of the Eastern Empire, to the Capture of Constantinople by the Turks, including the Rise and Progress of the Mohammedan Religion and the Crusades'.[36] Southey was a member of the Bristol Library Society and its records show that his borrowings included William Robertson's 1769 *History of the Reign of Charles V*, which of course included some discussion of the crusades.[37] In December 1798, Southey wrote to his longstanding friend, the financier John May:

'Dramatists and early novelists have ransacked early history and we have as many crusaders on the stage and in the circulating library as ever sailed to Palestine; but they only pay attention to the chronology and not to the manners or mind of the period'.[38]

We also know that his own library included a number of works about the crusades, including Fuller, Bongars, a presentation copy of Mills,[39] and several editions and translations of Tasso.[40]

There was some debate in the early 1800s about whether the term crusade should be applied to the early campaigns against Napoleon, but Southey, whose three-volume history of the Peninsula War was published between 1823 and 1832, certainly regarded this campaign as a 'crusade on the part of us and the Spaniards'.[41] He also noted the importance of the crusades in the history of Christianity in his 1820 *Life of Wesley*.[42]

Moreover, in a number of letters, Southey encouraged his younger brother Henry, a doctor, to write a history of the crusades:

> Some leisure hour, I will write to you vehemently about the crusades-being assured that you can in no way add so materially to your present enjoyment and future happiness, as by having some work of importance in hand and some pursuit of a higher nature than the ordinary ones of the world. You are well situated for books –many of these which are of most importance being at hand and you may make the whole skeleton of the work with your present stock of languages – it will be time enough at the end to incorporate Arabian documents if any of importance remain untranslated.[43]

And this was not just an idle exercise. Southey advised his brother which primary and secondary sources he should use and how to approach his subject:

> Read half a dozen authors at once, and thus you never need dwell upon one until you are tired of it; and begin the history of two or three crusades at once; that you may be able to go on with one part of the narrative when you are in want of materials for another. When you have done enough to give yourself security to yourself that you will do more, I will put in requisition all my means of obtaining books and borrow for you from Heber whatever his library contains.[44]

In another letter to John May, in November 1809, Southey expressed his delight that Harry: 'is going on well, and, to my great joy, is employing his leisure upon a History of the Crusades, a project which he long since formed, and in which I have good hope of his doing credit both to himself and his name'. Southey adds that he had talked to his brother about this and that Henry's wife gladly 'listened to me' and looked favourably upon his researches. He also recommended that Henry should consult Maimbourg, when he could find his history in a catalogue.[45]

There is no evidence that Henry's labours resulted in a published history. Perhaps his medical career, which culminated in an appointment as physician in ordinary to King George IV in 1823, allowed him insufficient time for such pursuits.[46] Nevertheless, the exchange of letters, advice about sources to consult, and reference to books borrowed from friends shed further light on contemporary attitudes to the crusades.

The amateur historian's interest in the subject is echoed, albeit humorously, in the literature of the day. In her novel *The Novice of Saint Dominick* published in 1806, Sydney Owenson (Lady Morgan) wrote that Lady Magdelaine de Montmoreil had spent 'four years in composing a voluminous history of the crusades, whether foreign or domestic, against infidel or apostate'.[47]

Southey's friend and fellow poet and writer Samuel Taylor Coleridge was also interested in the crusades. Growing up in the village of Ottery St Mary in Devon, he would have been familiar with the tomb of Sir Otho de Grandson, who accompanied Prince Edward on his crusade. As a journalist, Coleridge also entered the debate about whether the war against Napoleon deserved to be called a crusade. An article published in *The Courier* in August 1800 was titled 'The War Not a Crusade' and justified this judgement with a brief history of origins and the impact of the crusades themselves. Coleridge declared:

> Never was a war, in the best sense of the word, so holy; it is, perhaps, the only war in history in which defence by anticipation was no trick of Statesmen, but the demand of nations, the impulse of a general inspiration [...]. The Crusades were as favourable in their effects, as they were honourable in their causes. If therefore the present war be unnecessary in its origin, unprovoked in its primary movements, let us call it anything ONLY NOT A CRUSADE.[48]

William Morris

As someone who looked back to the Middle Ages as a golden era and called for a crusade against the current age, the Arts and Crafts designer William Morris was also interested in the history of the crusades. As a child, Morris is said to have worked his way through all of Scott's novels[49] and he was given a toy suit of armour for his eighth birthday.[50] In 1855, against the background of the Crimean War, when studying at Exeter College, Oxford, he was amongst those who submitted an entry for the Newdigate poetry prize on the subject of 'The Mosque Rising in the Temple of Solomon'. Morris did not win the prize but his poem, published much later, provides an insight into the sources that he consulted, from William of Tyre to Tasso, Michaud, and Gibbon.[51] As a poet, Morris wrote 'Riding Together' set against the background of Saint Louis's first crusade, which was published in the *Oxford and Cambridge Magazine* in 1856, and an episode from Joinville's history is said to have inspired *The Defence of Guinevere*. In 1893, Morris's Kelmscott Press also published William Caxton's translation of the *History of Godfroy of Bouloyne*. And other Arts and Crafts designers drew on the crusades as inspiration and subject matter for their works, in particular stained glass.[52]

There may also be another factor behind Morris's interest in the crusades. He had been a pupil at Marlborough School, and in 1848 the *Marlborough Magazine*, intended for pupils and those who had left the college in the previous two years, published an article by a CC on 'The Crusades: The Causes of Their Rise and Decline and Their Influence upon the Condition of Europe'. The Introduction states that the 'combination of religious and martial ardour' are 'without parallel in the history of the world'. The article concludes, however, that the long-term impact of the crusades was limited:

> If we accept that the impulse given to commerce and the improvement of society which naturally sprung from the circumstances of the case [...] perhaps no chapter of history exhibits a more stupendous record of the weakness of man and the futility of his efforts, than that which portrays the abortive results of the military enterprises of the twelfth and thirteenth centuries.[53]

This language seems to echo Oakeley's 1827 essay on *The Influence of the Crusades,* and perhaps this was available in the Marlborough School library.[54]

Sir James Mackintosh

Sir James Mackintosh was a very different reader. Born in Scotland in 1765, he studied medicine at Edinburgh University but was much preoccupied with contemporary politics and wrote *Vindiciae Gallicae* in defence of the French Revolution. He went on to study law and was appointed as a Judge in Bombay, India, in 1803. Whilst there, he was known for his extensive private library, which was augmented with regular additions chosen by his brother-in-law, a newspaper editor in London.[55] On his return to Britain in 1811, he became an MP and published a number of works of history.[56]

One finds glimpses of Mackintosh's extensive and varied reading in his letters and diaries, not least whilst he was making the lengthy journey to and from India. In March 1812, he wrote of his disappointment after reading Joinville, and in July 1817, he confessed that after working his way through Gibbon, 'instead of a treatise on Chivalry and Crusades, I exhibited a dignified and comic picture of them in Fairfax's Tasso and Don Quixote'. He also seems to have had an interest in the history of the Templars.[57]

In 1830, Mackintosh published a *History of England* as part of the Revd Dionysius Lardner's multi-volume *Cabinet Cyclopaedia,* which included references to the First and Third Crusades. Mackintosh devoted several pages to the history of the latter, quoting his primary sources in footnotes, and, as a lawyer, he addressed the argument of whether the crusades were just. He concluded:

> As every state may maintain its honour because it is essential to its safety, so Europe had a right to defend her common honour, which consisted materially in resisting or averting by chastisement, attacks on her common religion [...]. Wars to impose religion by force are the most execrable violation of the rights of mankind; wars to defend it are the most sacred exercise of these rights.[58]

General histories and collections

For many, such general histories of England and Europe would have been the main source of their knowledge of the crusades, and Mackintosh's history was widely reviewed. The historian and archivist Sir Francis Palgrave also devoted nearly 100 pages to the crusades in his *History of Normandy and England,* published in 1864. He drew parallels between the crusades and the modern colonial system but, unlike Alison and Mackintosh, Palgrave saw little long-term benefit and much evidence of cruelty and intolerance, recalling particularly the massacre at Jerusalem on the First Crusade:

> As there is always much alloy of evil in the good resulting from human exertions, so there is also a tincture of good usually granted

as an alleviation of evil. In this respect the crusades stand alone: we cannot discern any one resulting benefit which could compensate for their crimes. The crusades have no parallel. Every other state founded upon conquest has earned some worldly triumph, exhibiting the rougher virtues whereby the dominion was acquired, military skill, captainship, intelligence, grandeur; some period of unity, honour, splendour, prosperity. But Latin Jerusalem had none; never did she rise from her bath of polluted gore.[59]

The Revd Joseph Berington, a leading Catholic writer and author of *The Literary History of the Middle Ages*, published in 1811, shared the view that the crusades had produced little cultural or practical advantage: 'These expeditions were utterly sterile with respect to the arts, to learning, and to every moral advantage, and [...] they neither retarded the progress of the invading enemy, nor, for a single day, the fate of the Eastern empire'.[60] By contrast, Kenelm Digby, author of the four-volume *Broad Stone of Honour*, intended as a manual of chivalry, took issue with critics of the crusaders who quoted the arguments of Gibbon, Hume, and Robertson. Describing them as 'shallow praters and scribblers', he concluded:

It is much to be lamented that the acquaintance of the English reader with the characters and events of the Middle Ages should, for the most part, be derived from the writings of men, who were either infidels, or who wrote on every subject connected with religion, with the feelings and opinions of Scotch Presbyterian preachers of the last century; conscientious men no doubt, but certainly not the most enlightened estimators of Christianity or human nature.[61]

Digby was himself, of course, far from an objective commentator and two of his volumes took their titles from crusaders: Godefridus and Tancredus.

For those who preferred their history in bite-size chunks, there was a market for reprinting excerpts from longer histories in collections aimed at the general reader. For example, in 1880, Edward Gibbon's chapters on the crusades were published in the Chandos Classics series.[62] And compilers of popular histories, such as Charles Knight's *Half Hours of English History*, published in 1851, drew on a diverse range of sources. For the First Crusade, Knight selected an extract from David Hume's *History* but he then turned to the popular *Penny Magazine* for an account of Richard the Lionheart and the Third Crusade.[63] The crusades also featured in histories that took the form of letters, such as

Scott's *Tales of a Grandfather*, published in 1831 and intended for his grandson, John Hugh Lockhart.[64]

Encyclopaedias

Other readers would have gained their knowledge of the crusades from more general encyclopaedias. Mike Horswell has shown the evolution of attitudes to the crusades in articles published in the *Encyclopaedia Britannica*[65] and this period saw the publication of a range of single- and multi-volume encyclopaedias intended to appeal to various reading markets. In 1830, David Brewster began to publish his 18-volume *Edinburgh Encyclopaedia*, with an eight-page article on the crusades, which concluded, in language reminiscent of another Edinburgh resident, Hume, that even some positive benefits could not 'exculpate their authors from the charge of criminal ambition or enthusiastic folly'.[66] The Chambers brothers published an essay on the crusades in their *Miscellany of Useful and Entertaining Tracts* (1845 and 1847), as well as articles on the subject in the *Edinburgh Journal*, which was launched in 1832 and had a circulation of over 80,000.[67]

These examples illustrate the diversity and number of publications on the subject and the very different views that they articulated. In some cases, the authors wrote from a particular religious standpoint; in others they are making an historical judgement sometimes, but not always, influenced by contemporary events in the East, and this spectrum of views can be traced throughout the nineteenth century.[68]

Foreign publications

Debate and discussion were not confined to texts published in Britain or in English. One frequently cited work was the lecture on the character and effects of the crusades given at the Sorbonne in Paris in 1828 and later published in the *History of Civilization in Europe* by the French academic and statesman Francois Guizot. He argued that the crusades had laid some of the foundations of modern civilization: '[they] drew European society from a very straightened track and led it into new and infinitely more extensive paths; they commenced that transformation of the various elements of European society into governments and peoples, which is the character of modern civilization'.[69] Guizot's *History* was widely reviewed[70] and his lecture on the crusades was quoted both by one of the contributors (LA) to the 1870 debate in the *British Controversialist* and Archibald Alison. It was also available in several English translations, and the different backgrounds of the authors of these translations shed further light on reading practices in this period. They included the author and lawyer William Hazlitt, son of the famous essayist, and Priscilla Maria Beckwith, wife of a British Army general who fought in the Napoleonic wars in Spain, India, and Waterloo.

In 1861, Lucie, Lady Duff Gordon, who is perhaps better known for her *Letters from Egypt*, also published an English translation of Heinrich von Sybel's 1841 *Geschichte des ersten Krezzugs*, titled *The History and Literature of the Crusades*, which consisted of von Sybel's four lectures on the crusades and his analysis of the sources for the First Crusade.

Reviews of the publications of the Societe de L'Orient Latin could be found in, for example, the *Saturday Review*,[71] and the London-based *Foreign Quarterly Review*, which ran from 1827 to 1846 was established specifically to review books in other European languages known to British readers. Thus, in 1830, the *Review* published reviews of the histories of the crusades by Friedrich Wilken and Joseph Michaud.[72] The reviewer described the crusades as 'the most extraordinary phenomenon beyond question which the history of the world presents' and made clear his own analysis of the subject: 'He who reads or writes the History of the Crusades with feelings of contempt or aversion for those engaged in them, may be satisfied that he is yet far from possessing that calm comprehensive spirit of philosophy, without which history can never be read or written to advantage'. Of the two works under review, he preferred Wilken and dismissed the criticisms of the crusades to be found in Mills. The reviewer was also aware of earlier histories by Voltaire and Gibbon and the works of other French historians, such as Guizot.

Palgrave referred to both Wilken and Michaud in his account of the crusades[73] and such reviews may also have been the vehicle for some less assiduous readers, such as Charles Mackay, who included a lengthy chapter on the crusades in his book titled *Extraordinary Popular Delusions and the Madness of Crowds* to gain their knowledge of foreign publications.[74]

Conclusion

As the nineteenth century progressed, the British reader had access to a variety of primary sources and histories of the crusades, published not only in Britain but also elsewhere in Europe and not just restricted to English-language editions. These works were not only available for sale and in public and private libraries but also discussed in a range of weekly, monthly, and quarterly reviews and periodicals targeted at different audiences and published in London, Edinburgh, and other major cities. The crusades clearly remained a matter for debate, with wide-ranging views expressed in print and in both learned societies and local meetings. This was attributable in part to contemporary events, such as the massacre of Christians in Bulgaria in 1876 and the Greco–Turkish War of 1897, but the range of discussion is also evidence of genuine interest in the impact of the crusades and the national and international lessons to be learned from them.

Notes

1 See Tyerman, *The Debate*; Giles Constable, 'The Historiography of the Crusades' in *The Crusades from the Perspectives of Byzantium and the Muslim World*, eds. Angeliki E. Laiou and Roy Parviz Mottahedeh (Washington, DC, 2001), pp. 1–21; Siberry, *New Crusaders*, pp. 1–39.

2 For the variety of private libraries, see Murray Simpson, 'Private Libraries' in *The Edinburgh History of the Book in Scotland, 1707–1800*, eds. Stephen W. Brown and Warren McDougall (Edinburgh, 2012), pp. 313–26.

3 Robert Watt, *Bibliotheca or a General Index to British and Foreign Literature*, vol. 1 (Edinburgh, 1824), p. vi.

4 Siberry, 'The Crusades: The Nineteenth-Century Readers' Perspective' in *Engaging the Crusades*, eds. Mike Horswell and Jonathan Phillips (London, 2018), pp. 7–13.

5 Kathleen Hapgood, 'The Friends to Literature: Bristol Library Society 1772–1894', Avon Local History and Archaeology Publications 7 (2011).

6 The Bristol Library Society Registers, vols 26, 27, 28, 40, and 42 are preserved in the collection of the Central Library in Bristol. I am grateful to Dawn Dyer for her help in accessing this collection.

7 I am grateful to Lara Haggerty, the librarian at Innerpeffray, for sending me details of these borrowing records.

8 Joseph Francois Michaud, *Histoire des croisades illustree de 100 grand compositions par Gustave Dore* (Paris, 1877). For example, *The Departure* shows a family huddled around the base of a cross in prayer as, in the distance, watched by his wife carrying a young child, a knight departs on crusade, complementing the text on the impact of the crusades in Europe. In *The Return*, a crusader on horseback approaches a similar family group and cross, with their castle in the distance (pp. 294–6).

9 Dan Malan, *Gustave Dore. A Comprehensive Biography and Bibliography* (St Louis, MO, 1995), pp. 137–9. A review in the *Dublin University Magazine* 90 (1877) pp. 508–9, commenting on the depiction of the slaughter at the battle of Dorylaeum, drew a link with more recent loss of life in Bulgaria, 'the terror of artillery having been added to all the deathly enginery of the crusaders'.

10 Julian Treuherz, *Victorian Painting* (London, 1993), p. 24.

11 See Siberry, *New Crusaders*, pp. 161–75.

12 Jon P. Klancher, *The Making of the English Reading Audiences 1790–1832* (Madison, WI, 1987), p. ix, and Alvin Sullivan, ed., *British Literary Magazines–The Victorian and Edwardian Age 1837–1913* (London, 1985), p. xiii.

13 Gillian Williamson, *English Masculinity in the Gentleman's Magazine 1731–1815* (Basingstoke, UK, 2016), p. 69.

14 Walter E. Houghton, ed., *The Wellesley Index to Victorian Periodicals 1824–1900* (Toronto, 1966), p. 1.

15 See Tyerman, *Debate*, pp. 98–100.

16 *The Spectator*, 11 May 1844, p. 16.

17 Blackwoods was founded in 1824 to present a different viewpoint from the liberal Whig *Edinburgh Magazine*.

18 Alison, 'The Crusades', pp. 475–92. The essay was subsequently included in Alison's *Essays Political, Historical and Miscellaneous* (Edinburgh, 1850), pp. 347–75. A rather different analysis of Michaud's history and the crusades appeared in *The North British Review*, also published in Edinburgh, in 1844.

19 Houghton, *Wellesley Index*, vol. 4, pp. 114–25.

20 See the entry for Hannah Lawrance in the *Oxford Dictionary of National Biography* (henceforth, ODNB), <odnb.com>, [accessed 20 October 2020].

21 Hannah Lawrance, 'The Crusades as Described by Crusaders', *British Quarterly Review*, 18 (1853), pp. 63–101.

22 'Were the Crusades Beneficial to Social Progress'. *The British Controversialist, and Literary Magazine* (London, 1870), pp. 128–31, 290–5, 359–65, 449–53.

23 Ibid., pp. 128–9.

24 *The Debater's Handbook of Controversial Topics* (London, 1868), p. 20.

25 *The British Controversialist* (London, 1870), p. 359.

26 Lady Knightley of Fawsley, *Politics and Society: The Journals of Lady Knightley of Fawsley 1885–1913*, ed. Peter Gordon (Northampton, UK, 1999). Lady Knightley was a prominent women's activist and member of the Order of St John. See Siberry, *New Crusaders*, p. 108. Lord Wolseley was a senior British general who had served in the Crimean War, India, and the Sudan.

27 *The Cambrian Newspaper*, 29 January 1897, p. 3.

28 Saladin, 'The Crusades', *Secular Review* (1884), pp. 3–14. This was subsequently printed as a pamphlet. See also Alastair Bonnett, 'The Agnostic Saladin', *History Today* (2013), pp. 47–52, and Valerie E. Chancellor, *History for their Masters: Opinion in British History Textbooks 1800–1914* (Bath, UK, 1970), pp. 23–4.

29 This preceded the article on the crusades in Saladin's *The Crusades: Their Reality and Romance* (London, 1885).

30 F. Damiani, 'Memoir on the Vicissitudes of the Principality of Antioch, during the Crusades', *Archaeologia* 15 (1806), pp. 234–63.

31 *Saturday Review*, 'Modern Crusades', 29 September 1869, pp. 377–8; 'A Forgotten Crusade: The Conquest of Lisbon', 14 April 1888, pp. 439–40; 'Joinville and Saint Louis', 10 March 1866, pp. 297–9; 'The Finances of the

Crusades', 13 October 1877, pp. 455–6; 'Saladin in Cairo', 1882, pp. 792–3; and 'The Eastern Question', 12 January 1876, pp. 35–6.

32 *Edinburgh Review* 179 (1894), pp. 158–79. For Conder's colonialist approach to crusade history, see Ronnie Ellenblum, *Crusader Castles and Modern Histories* (Cambridge, UK, 2007), pp. 47–8.

33 Siberry, 'Readers' Perspective', pp. 13–16.

34 Robert Southey, *The Collected Letters of Robert Southey*, eds. Lynda Pratt, Tim Fulford, and Ian Packer, <www.romantic-circles.org>, [accessed 20 October 2020]. Letter to John May, 26 July 1820.

35 William A. Speck, *Robert Southey: Entire Man of Letters* (New Haven, CT, 2006), p. 12. Southey later acquired the complete works of Tasso. See *Letters*, 14 August 1836 and 31 July 1819. He also referred to a romance of Richard Coeur de Lion in his commonplace book.

36 Unfortunately the text of the lecture has not survived. It was one of 12 lectures covering the range of British, European, and American history and tickets were sold through a local bookseller. For the background to the lectures, see Stuart Andrews, 'Southey, Coleridge and Islam', *The Wordsworth Circle* 46 (2015), pp. 109–16.

37 Paul Kaufman, 'The Reading of Southey and Coleridge: The Record of Their Borrowing from the Bristol Library, 1793–98', *Modern Philology* 2 (1923–4), pp. 317–20.

38 Letter to John May, 14 December 1798. He also wrote to his Westminster school friend, Grosvenor Charles Bedford, on 17 November 1808, 'I love and vindicate the crusades'.

39 Southey was critical of Mills's work and, in a letter, described it as 'one of the worst books in my possession'. Letter to John May, 9 February 1828.

40 *Catalogue of the Valuable Library of the Late Robert Southey* (London, 1844), items 1189, 1193, 1948, and 2775–9. The sale lasted 16 days and raised nearly £3,000.

41 Letter to Grosvenor Bedford, 17 November 1808.

42 Robert Southey, *The Life of Wesley and the Rise and Progress of Methodism*, vol. 1 (London, 1820), p. 310.

43 Letter to Henry Southey, 18 July 1809.

44 Ibid. Richard Heber was a noted bibliophile and friend of Southey.

45 Letter to Henry Southey, 8 August 1809.

46 See the ODNB entry for Henry Southey, <odnb.com>, [accessed 20 October 2020].

47 Sydney Owenson, *The Novice of Saint Dominick* (London, 1806), p. 1.

48 Samuel Coleridge, *Essays on His Times in 'The Morning Post' and 'The Courier'*, ed. David V. Erdman, vol. 11 (Princeton, NJ, 1978), pp. 240–2.

49 Fiona MacCarthy, *William Morris: A Life for Our Time* (London, 1995), p. 5.

50 Edward and Stephanie Godwin, *Warrior Bard: The Life of William Morris* (London, 1947), p. 5.

51 William Whitla, 'William Morris's "The Mosque Rising in the Place of the Temple of Solomon": A Critical Text', *Pre-Raphaelite Studies* 9 (2000), pp. 43–81.

52 See Siberry, 'Saint Louis: A Crusader King and Hero for Victorian and First World War Britain and Ireland' in *Engaging the Crusades: The Making of Crusading Heroes and Villains* (London, 2020), pp. 101–2.

53 *Marlborough Magazine*, April 1848, pp. 113–24.

54 See Tyerman, *Debate*, p. 120.

55 Graham Shaw, 'India', in *The Edinburgh History of the Book: Ambition and Industry, 1800–80*, vol. 3, ed. Bill Bell (Edinburgh, 2007), p. 460.

56 See the ODNB entry for James Mackintosh, <odnb.com>, [accessed 20 October 2020].

57 Robert J. Mackintosh, ed., *Memoirs of the Life of Sir James Mackintosh*, 2nd ed. (London, 1836), vol. 1, pp. 291, 448; vol. 2, p. 229.

58 James Mackintosh, *History of England* (London, 1830), vol. 1, pp. 124–6.

59 Francis Palgrave, *The Collected Historical Works of Sir Francis Palgrave* (Cambridge, UK, 1921), vol. 4, p. 332.

60 Joseph Berington, *The Literary History of the Middle Ages* (London, 1846), p. 269.

61 Kenelm Digby, *The Broad Stone of Honour, The True Sense and Practice of Chivalry: Tancredus* (London, 1828), p. 45, n. 54.

62 Edward Gibbon, *The Life and Letters of Edward Gibbon with His History of the Crusades* (London, 1880), pp. 359–483.

63 *Half Hours of English History* selected and arranged by Charles Knight (London, 1851), pp. 174–7, 273–8.

64 Walter Scott, *Tales of a Grandfather: Being Stories Taken from the History of France* (Edinburgh, 1831). The epistolary form had also been used by William Russell, *The History of Modern Europe* (London, 1814). He described the crusades as 'romantic expeditions, though barbarous and destructive in themselves, [...] followed by some important consequences [...] conducive to the welfare of the community and the individual', vol. 1, p. 376.

65 Mike Horswell, 'From "Superstitious Veneration" to "War to Defend Christendom": The Crusades in the *Encyclopaedia Britannica* 1771–2018' in *The Legacy of the Crusades: History and Memory*, eds. Torben K. Nielsen and Kurt V. Jensen (Turnhout, Belgium, forthcoming).

66 David Brewster, ed., *Edinburgh Encyclopaedia* (Edinburgh, 1830), vol. 7, pp. 375–83.

67 See *Edinburgh Journal* (1834), pp. 219–20 and (1848), pp. 310–12.

68 For example, the crusades merited some 200 pages in Samuel Jacob's *History of the Ottoman Empire, Including a Survey of the Greek Empire and the Crusades* (London, 1854). The Preface drew a link between the medieval expeditions and the Crimean War: 'the deep interest now so universally felt in the fate of Turkey, linked as that fate has become with the interests of civilization throughout the world, has led the publishers to use every effort to make this treatise as comprehensive as possible'.

69 Francois Guizot, *History of Civilization in Europe* (Oxford, 1837), pp. 145–61. Some of Guizot's contemporaries were less positive about the crusades. See Ceri Crossley, *French Historians and Romanticism. Thierry, Guizot, the*

Saint Simonians, Quinet and Michelet (London, 1993). Guizot was also an avid reader of Scott's novels.

70　A review in the *Gentleman's Magazine* (1846), pp. 167–8, commented that Guizot's views on the crusades were 'particularly luminous'.

71　*Saturday Review*, 19 July 1884, pp. 81–2. See also *The Academy,* 16 February 1884, pp. 113–14.

72　*Foreign Quarterly Review* (1830), pp. 623–54.

73　Palgrave, *Collected Historical Works*, p. 318.

74　Charles Mackay, *Memoirs of Extraordinary Popular Delusions* (London, 1841), pp. 354–461. The book ran to several editions and the crusades chapter was printed separately in 1854. For analysis of Mackay's sources, see James Muldoon, 'Mad Men on Crusade: Religious Madness and the Origins of the First Crusade' in *Seven Myths of the Crusades*, eds. Alfred J. Andrea and Andrew Holt (Indianapolis, IN, 2015), pp. 32–3. See also Siberry, *New Crusaders*, pp. 29–30.

2   Finding crusaders
Physical monuments and discoveries

In the sixteenth century, John Leland and William Camden had laid the foundations of recorded county history, but interest in the subject increased in the seventeenth and eighteenth centuries with the publication of county histories, such as William Dugdale's *Antiquities of Warwickshire* published in 1656, and with the establishment of national, county, and local antiquarian and archaeological societies and associated publications.[1] By the early nineteenth century, there were detailed illustrated publications of church monuments by antiquarians, such as Richard Gough and Charles Stothard,[2] and studies of medieval armour by collectors, such as Sir Samuel Meyrick.[3] There were also lively exchanges of correspondence about recent archaeological discoveries and historical and genealogical research, with detailed papers on these subjects presented to national and local groups. History was therefore both visible and a 'live' subject of debate and discussion.

I will discuss the way in which this stimulated interest in family crusaders in the next chapter, but there was also great interest in physical monuments related to or said to relate to the crusades. These could (and still can) be found in almost every county in Britain, and the stories associated with them have developed over the centuries, along with the ways in which such monuments have been understood and interpreted. In the nineteenth century in particular, archaeological excavations and church restorations revealed new items of interest, and there were public exhibitions throughout Britain, not least of course the Great Exhibition of 1851, attended by some 6 million people. And even if some of the evidence on which the attributions were based does not meet modern research standards, it is a further aspect of the memory of the crusades. These physical monuments, as much as the written word, which was the subject of the previous chapter, have had a key role to play in shaping the national memory of the crusades and inspiring stories of crusading endeavours over the centuries.

The crossed-legs effigy

The most frequently cited monuments linked with the crusades are of course the crossed-legs effigies to be found in many parish churches in Britain.[4] The argument that this pose reflected participation in the crusades can be found in numerous histories from the late sixteenth century onwards and was reinforced by the thirteenth-century effigies in the Temple Church in London. Many visited this church, and its restoration in the 1840s spawned a series of well-illustrated scholarly and popular publications.[5] Plaster casts of the effigies were also on display at Crystal Palace in 1851.[6]

In fact, the recumbent crossed-legs style was simply a fashion between the mid-thirteenth and fourteenth centuries, but it is a 'myth' that has proved very difficult to dispel. Conscious of their readers' appetite for ancestral tales of noble endeavours, the compilers of early county histories were keen to record the tombs of those they believed to have been crusaders[7] and, if some have challenged the view, there were (and are) many others who have repeated and reinforced it.

In 1830, the author of a letter to the editor of the *Gentleman's Magazine* about a crossed-legs effigy at St Mary's Church, Brading, on the Isle of Wight, declared 'there are no cross-legged monumental effigies which can be identified with any other persons than those who had either undertaken or performed the crusade', but he was soon challenged by another correspondent, who pointed out that many such figures belonged to a period 'subsequent to the last crusade'.[8] There was also correspondence in the magazine about an effigy discovered at Botus Fleming, near Saltash in Cornwall, with the correspondent noting that, because the effigy had crossed-legs, 'the villagers have given it the name of the Crusader's tomb and imagine that its occupant was the founder of their church or at least a great benefactor to it'.[9]

These effigies evoked memories of past heroic deeds and, in his 1846 essay on the crusades, Archibald Alison wrote: 'No monument is yet approached by the generous and brave with such emotion as those now mouldering in our churches, which represent the warrior lying with his arms crossed on his breast, in token that, during life, he had served in the Holy Wars'.[10] Parallels were also drawn between such effigies and soldiers engaged in the First World War. In July 1916, a letter to the magazine *Country Life* made an explicit link between monuments in a

Kent country church believed to commemorate medieval crusaders and those fighting across the English Channel:

> Within the walls crowded memories of local knights and squires of long ago. Crusaders in recumbent effigies, and their story marked in crumbling stone and brass. In the porch lists hang the village roll of honour, from manor, rectory and cottage alike, and some names recall the family traditions of the old Crusades.[11]

In December 1917, a descendant of a local knight believed to have been a crusader from Crickhowell, in Breconshire, sent a wreath of laurels to be placed upon his tomb in celebration of the occupation of Jerusalem by British forces. In his sermon, the local rector noted that more than 600 years before, a local knight had gone to fight 'for the deliverance of Palestine' and others were now fighting and had lost their lives 'in the same mission'.[12] The family of Captain Charles Grant Seely, who was killed in action in the second battle of Gaza in 1917, asked the sculptor Sir Thomas Brock to design a crossed-legs effigy in the parish church of Gatcombe on the Isle of Wight in his memory. To underline the link with the crusades, Seely's parents also commissioned a set of curtains (now lost) in 'cloth of gold on which are figures of the crusaders'.[13]

Even today, church guidebooks, drawing on earlier antiquarian histories, claim that crossed-legs effigies represent a local crusader, and the same attributions can be found in numerous county histories.[14] Some writers have also suggested that children born in the Holy Land were commemorated in this way.[15]

Tennyson and Wordsworth helped to perpetuate the myth by writing poems about a 'crusader's tomb',[16] and the artist William Etty claimed that his picture of Godfrey of Bouillon (now in the Manchester City Art Gallery) had been influenced by 'the tomb of a crusader which I sketched in chainmail' at Howden Church in Yorkshire.[17] The small crossed-legs effigy in Purbeck marble at Netley Abbey in Hampshire, now moved to the parish church, may also have inspired the gothic novel *Netley Abbey*, published by the Revd Richard Warner in 1795, in which the hero of the tale, Baron Villars, takes part in the crusade of Lord Edward.[18]

Although his son, Francis Turner Palgrave, later included a poem, 'The Crusader's tomb', in his *Visions of England*, published in 1881, the historian Francis Palgrave was quite clear in his dismissal of such romantic ideas:

One hardly knows where to begin in developing and dispelling the unrealities. You contemplate the cross-legged effigy, grim in mailed armour-you call him a crusader. Could the statue open its mouth and speak, the first thing the stone would say is 'No, friend, the bones which lie beneath me belong not to a crusader.' The notion that the attitude symbolizes the doughty deeds of the Holy Land is a thorough figment; an antiquarian conceit, which has ripened into a vulgar error.[19]

The link with the crusades, however, continued to be made, and its longevity matters because these effigies were a very tangible link with the crusading past, not only for the proud descendants of those commemorated but also for their local communities. They were also an ever-present illustration of an important chapter in the nation's history about which they might have read or learned at school.

Family tales

The noble deeds performed by an ancestral crusader could also be seen depicted in historic houses. In an early poem, Lord Byron, who was a great admirer of the work of Tasso, referred to an ancestor, John of Horiston, who had fought at Ascalon.[20] At Byron's home, Newstead Abbey, figures depicting a Saracen were said to reflect a story of a crusader's rescue of a Christian lady, and in 1824 the American author Washington Irving described the carvings in his room at Newstead:

> The most curious relique of old times, however, in this quaint apartment was a great chimney piece of panel work carved in high relief, with niches or compartments, each containing human busts that protruded almost entirely from the wall. Some of the figures were in ancient Gothic garb; the most striking among them was a female, who was earnestly regarded by a fierce Saracen from an adjoining niche [...]. Some suppose it to illustrate an adventure in the Holy Land, and that the lady in effigy has been rescued by some crusader of the family from the turbaned Turk who watches her so earnestly.[21]

Irving was a humorous observer of old British customs and stories, and one example shows how they often developed with the telling. In *Old Christmas*, illustrated by the artist Randolph Caldecott, Irving described a festive stay with the owner of Bracebridge Hall, said to be an amalgam of country houses that he had visited.[22] In the village church, the narrator is shown an effigy of a crusader:

> Just beside the altar was a tomb of ancient workmanship, in which lay the effigy of a warrior in armour, with his legs crossed, a sign of his having been a crusader. I was told that it was one of the family who had signalised himself in the Holy Land, and the same whose picture hung over the fireplace in the hall.

This ancestral portrait was duly decorated for the Christmas festivities, as were a helmet and weapons on the opposite wall that were said to be the arms of the crusader. The narrator adds:

> I must own, by the by, I had strong doubts about the authenticity of the painting and armour as having belonged to the crusader, they certainly having the stamp of more recent days; but I was told that the painting had been considered time out of mind, and that as to the armour, it had been found in a lumber room, and elevated to its present situation by the squire, who at once determined it to be the armour of the family hero; and as he was absolute authority on all such subjects in his own household, the matter had passed into current acceptation.

The imaginative squire also regaled his guests with stories of the crusader getting up from his tomb and walking around the village and there was even a hint of buried treasure.[23]

On a visit to Westminster Abbey, Irving also reflected on the tomb of a knight in armour, which he concluded, again because of the crossed legs, had been a crusader: 'There is something extremely picturesque in the tombs of these adventurers [...] they are like objects from some strange and distant land, of which we have no certain knowledge, and about which all our conceptions are vague and visionary'.[24] Whilst Irving's description is a deliberate caricature, it reflects the interest in the subject and the popularity of such claims.[25] And in 1839, the Conservative politician Viscount Sandon, son of the first Earl of Harrowby, was satirized in the radical *Chartist* magazine for his claims of noble and crusading lineage:

> He concentrated in himself all sorts of historic associations; had a remote grandfather who was an intimate of some ancestor of William of Normandy, has a family vault full of mouldering dust

of men who have worn coat armour [...]. He has without doubt, somewhere or other, a church full of monuments of cross legged knights, and can tell when and where the man who handed down to him his name and lands fought by the side of lion-hearted Richard, and pushed back at their lance's point hosts of swarming Saracens.[26]

Tombs of crusaders

Other church monuments linked with crusaders can be found in counties throughout Britain, with their stories chronicled in published histories, even if participation in the crusades cannot be fully substantiated by modern research.[27] Three examples from Somerset, North Wales, and Surrey illustrate the range and geographical spread of crusade stories and their visibility to proud family, neighbours, and visitors to the area.

Sir Richard Perceval: Weston Giordano, Somerset

In the churchyard of Weston Giordano in Somerset, there is a chest tomb (reputedly the oldest in England and, until the depredations of the Civil War, surmounted by a canopy and with brass decorations) with the inscription: 'Orate pro anima Rycardi Perceval qui militavit in terra sancta com Rege Ricardi AD MCXC' [pray for the soul of Richard Perceval who fought in the Holy Land with King Richard 1190] (Figure 2.1). The Sir Richard Perceval thus commemorated is said to have fought bravely with Richard the Lionheart on the Third Crusade

Figure 2.1 Tomb of Sir Richard Perceval, Weston Giordano
Source: Author's photo.

and is recorded in James Cruikshank Dansey's list of English crusaders published in 1850:[28]

> Sir Richard Percival of Stawel and Weston in Girdano attended King Richard in the Third Crusade. Tradition reports that, having lost his leg in an engagement, he still continued the combat till he lost an arm; and even then remained undauntingly on horseback till he fell from loss of blood. This is doubtless the origin of the family crest-a knight on horseback with one leg couped.

In spite of these wounds, Sir Richard is said to have returned home and died in about 1202.

Authenticating this story, like many others, is more problematic. Perceval does not appear in the standard chronicles for the Third Crusade,[29] and Dansey only cites as his source an unnamed History of Somerset. The Revd John Collinson's *History and Antiquities of the County of Somerset Collected from Authentick Records*, published in 1791, however, does include this tale, adding that Perceval was accompanied on his crusade by his son, another Richard. The story can also be traced further back to a history of the family by James Anderson, which was commissioned by the ninth Earl of Egmont and published in 1742. Anderson cites as his source 'Josephus Iscanus, who was with him [Richard] in the same war, in the office of secretary to the king, and wrote a particular account of that enterprise'.[30] Josephus Iscanus was in fact Joseph of Exeter, a nephew of Archbishop Baldwin of Canterbury, who accompanied him on the Third Crusade. A notable Latin poet, Joseph composed an epic poem on the Trojan War and a now lost poem on the Third Crusade.[31] This is presumably the source in question, but in the sixteenth century, Leland could only find a fragment, so the sourcing puzzle for the Perceval story remains.

Sir Richard's courage appears, however, to have been much admired in family circles in the mid-seventeenth century. According to an account by the local vicar, quoted by Anderson:

> The veneration of him continued so strong with his descendants, that James Perceval of Weston-Gordein (father of Thomas, the last male of that line, who died about the year 1641) upon his deathbed and almost in his last agonies, entreated his family, that they should not omit to comply with his last request, which was to lay his body in the same tomb with that of this Richard his ancestor, that his ashes might mingle with those of his glorious predecessor.[32]

Richard Perceval also features in the epic poem *Coeur de Lion or the Third Crusade*, composed by Eleanor Porden, the first wife of the explorer Sir John Franklin, and published in 1822.[33]

It does not actually matter whether there is clear evidence that Sir Richard was a member of the Third Crusade. The way in which the story has persisted and developed through the centuries shows the importance of the crusades in this family's history dating back to at least the 1600s. The strength of the continuing family tradition and pride is reflected in a stained-glass window at the West end of the church (Figure 2.2), designed by Jane Perceval in 1908. It depicts Ascelin, the founder of the church and son of a follower of William the Conqueror; James, a sixteenth-century church benefactor; and in the left light the crusader Richard. The family motto is *sub cruce candida* (under the white cross) and their coat of arms has three white maltese crosses on a red background.

Figure 2.2 Window, Weston Giordano Church
Source: Author's photo.

Gruffydd ap Llewellyn ap Ynyr of Ial: Llanarmon Dyffryn Ceiriog

Another story of crusade courage and heroism concerned Gruffydd ap Llewellyn ap Ynyr of Ial, the brother of Llewellyn the Bishop of St Asaph in North Wales, who was said to have fought on heroically in an unspecified siege during the crusades, even after receiving a serious wound in his abdomen exposing his intestines, which a dog then started to devour. The gory, if unlikely, story is depicted on his effigy, which was once at Valle Crucis Abbey in Denbighshire, but is now at Llanarmon Church and can be traced back at least to the mid-eighteenth century. Apart from accounts in travel guides, it was discussed in several volumes of *Archaeologia Cambrensis*, the journal of the Cambrian Archaeological Association, as well as the weekly Welsh newspaper *Y Gwyliedydd*, and must therefore have been well known not just in the immediate locality.[34] Similar tales of heroism on crusade can be found in other local, county, and national archaeological journals.

Symbols of crusading

The heraldry associated with crusading will be discussed in Chapter 4, but symbols associated with participation on the crusades were also displayed on church monuments.

The Cobham family

The tombs of the Lords Cobham, in Lingfield Church in Surrey, are just one example of this. The heraldry of the Cobhams, who held land in Kent and Surrey and served Henry III and the three King Edwards as soldiers and administrators, included a Saracen's head, which was said to denote a crusading ancestor. In an article published in *Archaeologia Cantiana* in 1877, John G. Waller wrote of Henry de Cobham, who died c. 1225: 'It is said that he was one of the crusaders present at the siege of Acre in 1191. Of this fact, perhaps, the crest of the Saracen's head, which was borne equally by both of the families who descended from him, was a memento'.[35] This link with the crusades is still repeated in a framed manuscript note on the pillar above the tomb of Reginald, 1st Lord Cobham, who died in 1361, but no Cobham can be found in the sources for the Third Crusade, and recent research by Nigel Saul has identified a rather different justification for the choice of heraldic symbol:

Three of Edward's most distinguished captains – two of them knights of the Garter – made use of crests with Saracen's heads. These were Sir Miles Stapleton, Reginald, Lord Cobham and John de Vere, Earl of Oxford [...]. The Saracen disguise was a very popular one in mid fourteenth century [...]. It is not unreasonable to suppose that Stapleton, Cobham and Oxford had all fought at some stage as members of a Saracen team in court entertainments. The appearance of the Saracen crest on such later monuments is probably to be explained in these terms: the knights commemorated had at some stage, perhaps in their youths or between campaigns, served in tourneying teams.[36]

Archaeological discoveries and debates

Antiquarian excavations and research also uncovered artefacts associated, or said to be associated, with the crusades, from the tiles at Chertsey Abbey in Surrey depicting Richard and Saladin[37] to skeletons of possible crusaders. Accounts of these discoveries were often published in local and national journals, thus raising much more than local interest and feeding the nineteenth-century appetite for tales of noble deeds to embellish and enrich later family pride and position.

Two examples, from Cumbria and Dorset, show the interest such discoveries aroused and how stories could develop over time, as well as their geographical spread.

Udard de Broham

In October 1846, some workmen repairing the vault of the Brougham family in Ninekirks Church in Cumbria uncovered a skeleton, buried with crossed legs with an iron spur around the left heel, beneath an incised slab. The tomb also contained a fragment of glass that appeared to be of eastern origin. In an article published in *Medieval Archaeology* in 1847, William Brougham, who later became Lord Brougham, stated that the tomb was known to the family as the crusader's tomb and assigned to Udard de Broham, who had been on the Second Crusade. Udard is said to have flourished between 1140 and 1185, but there is no first-hand evidence of his crusading. Whether or not the skeleton was of a crusader, the family seems to have been proud of its forebear. The skull and spur were apparently kept at Brougham Castle and shown to favoured guests, and the family is also said to have had the crusader's shirt of mail and sword on display in their armoury.[38]

Visitors to the Castle were certainly told this tale, and one account prompted a lively exchange in the *Gentleman's Magazine*. A George Shaw, from Saddleworth, near Manchester, repeated the family stories in a letter published in April 1848, but a reader signing himself as Old Subscribers dismissed the crusading claim in forthright terms:

> As to the crusader's grave, so wonderfully discovered in the parish church of Brougham, belonging to Udard de Broham, it is the most puerile creation ever set up, particularly as the bones bear no inscriptions nor dates; and it was shrewdly observed by one of the London papers at the time of the supposed discovery, that from the cross-legged position in which the skeleton was found it was as likely to have been the timbers of an ancient knight of the thimble as a crusader. We are of the same opinion.[39]

Lord Brougham is said to have admitted, himself, that his forebears were of more modest origins,[40] but it remained a good story to tell visitors. One such occasion was described by one of his biographers, Lord Campbell:

> In the church at Brougham there was the grave of an Edward de Broham, who accompanied Richard I to the Holy Land and fought many stout battles against the Saracens. My noble and learned friend (the Lord Chancellor, Lord Brougham) lately opened his coffin, brought away the skull and placed it in his baronial hall, under the purse, which contained the Great Seal of England. Being called upon to admire the grinning crusader, I could only say that I was much struck by the family likeness between him and his illustrious descendant [...] particularly in the lengthiness of the jaw.[41]

The Stock Gaylard crusader

In 1884, the children of Mr and Mrs Harry Yeatman decided to restore the Church of St Barnabas, Stock Gaylard in Dorset, in their parents' memory. Beneath a stone effigy of a crossed-legs knight, known to the family the Knight Templar effigy, they found a dismembered skeleton and some scraps of red leather. Contemporary notes by Lewys Legge Yeatman speculated that the Templar's bones were brought back from Palestine in a leather case. They also described a ceremony, attended by the family, in which the bones were placed in a new wooden coffin bearing a red Templar cross in a burial service on Sunday, 31 August 1884.[42] The estate website suggests, without further detail, that the bones belonged to Sir Ingelramus de Waleys, Lord of the Manor, who was said to have died fighting in Jerusalem in 1274. A tree in the grounds of Stock Gaylard manor is also referred to as the crusader's tree and believed to date to the Middle Ages.[43] Rather appropriately, a bronze memorial plaque on the opposite wall of the church commemorates another member of the family, Captain Harry Farr Yeatman of the Dorset Yeomanry, who died during the Palestine campaign in November 1917, a month before the capture of Jerusalem.

Heart burials

A number of monuments said to contain or commemorate the heart of a crusader were also discovered in this period.

The Leybourne heart

In 1830, work on the north wall of the north aisle of Leybourne Church in Kent revealed a niche with two chapel-shaped shrines, one of which contained a lead cylindrical box enclosing an embalmed heart (Figure 2.3). This aroused much local interest and was the subject of an article in *Archaeologia Cantiana* by a local vicar and antiquarian, Revd

Figure 2.3 Heart Shrine, Leybourne Church
Source: Author's photo.

Lambert Blackwell Larking.[44] Larking wrote that the heart belonged to Sir Roger de Leybourne, who had accompanied Prince Edward on his crusade: 'For myself, I am convinced that the heart of the crusader, the friend and companion of Prince Edward, the great Sir Roger de Leyburn, is deposited here, as though the fact were actually declared by an inscription carved upon the shrine'.[45] Sir Roger did not actually take part in the crusade, dying in Gascony in 1271 whilst raising troops for the expedition, but his heart was returned to the church where he had founded a chantry. The second recess was probably intended for his wife but was not used when she remarried.[46]

The practice of dividing the body, with the heart and entrails buried separately, was not unusual[47] and this is not the only example of a heart burial associated with the crusades. William de Percy, who died during the siege of Jerusalem in the First Crusade, is said to have been buried at Montjoie outside Jerusalem, but a sixteenth-century poem claimed that his heart was brought back to England and buried at the Abbey of Whitby, to which he had donated substantial land holdings.[48] The family of Sir Philip D'Aubigny, who was buried in the Holy Sepulchre in Jerusalem, also believed that his heart had been returned to England and preserved in Wells Cathedral, in his home county of Somerset.[49] For crusaders who had died in the Holy Land, the burial of some physical remains back home, whether fact or creative fiction, was a means of underlining their noble service and enhancing family prestige or the reputation of an associated religious foundation.[50]

Such monuments could take a variety of forms. An unusual shield-shaped monument with two hands clutching a heart in St Giles's Church, Bredon, Worcestershire, is known as the crusader's tomb, and St Mary's Church in Chirk, in North Wales, has a small gravestone depicting a figure carrying a heart that was found in the churchyard in the nineteenth century and is said again to represent a deceased crusader (Figure 2.4).[51]

Whether or not such stories can be substantiated, they remain part of local history and thereby form part of the collective memory of the crusades. The nineteenth-century interest in the subject was reflected in book by Emily Sophia Hartshorne, published privately in 1861 and titled *Enshrined Hearts of Warriors*, which begins with a description of the crusades under the heading, 'The Sacred Enterprise'. Hartshorne concludes with a romanticized description of the crusader's wife receiving the heart of a deceased holy warrior:

> Knights and squires became the bearers of these precious relics to
> the bereaved wife or child, to be by their loving hands deposited in
> some sacred spot endeared to the departed hero, there to remind

Figure 2.4 Crusader Memorial, Chirk Church
Source: Author's photo.

them of his lingering presence, until the time should come when this small portion of his mortal frame might finally rest with theirs at their own decease.[52]

The rather gruesome story of the fate that befell a crusader's heart in the hands of a jealous husband also inspired a poem published in 1895. It told the story of how he tricked his wife into eating the heart of her suspected lover, which had been brought home from the Holy Land by his loyal squire.[53]

Arms and armour

There was also a lively antiquarian interest in the study and display of medieval armour with, for example, Sir Samuel Meyrick's *Critical Inquiry into Antient Armour*, published in 1824. Meyrick's own collection of armour (much of it now in the Wallace Collection in London) was on display both at Goodrich Court in Herefordshire and at his London home and was said by one visitor to include items relating to the crusades.[54]

Meyrick's work was founded on detailed research, but some attributions of crusade armour were less soundly based. One such example was the mail-clad figure, mounted on an armoured horse, known as the Norman Crusader, on display at the Tower of London from 1833. It has a curious history, which reflects the fascination with medieval artefacts and their variable attribution.

The 'crusader' is first recorded as part of a museum in Lichfield, Staffordshire, formed by Richard Greene, a local apothecary. Greene's collection was open to the public every day of the week except Sunday and was a popular attraction in the second half of the eighteenth century. He is said to have acquired his crusader from Tong Castle in Shropshire, the home of the Pembrugge family, when the castle hall was being spring-cleaned: 'The hauberk and mail legging, stiffened with bacon fat and dust, were thrown down as valueless. Greene softened them before a great fire and was then permitted to remove them to his museum, apparently as a gift of the Revd Thomas Buckridge, vicar of Tong'. The armour was also illustrated in the antiquarian Francis Grose's treatise on armour published in 1785.[55]

After Greene's death in 1793, William Bullock, a Liverpool goldsmith, purchased his collection of arms and armour, and the crusader featured prominently in his museum. In 1809, Bullock transferred his collection to London and by 1816, the collection had passed to a Mr Gwennap, who put it on display in the Oplotheca in Lower Brook Street where it was seen by many, including Sir Walter Scott. It was also depicted in engravings in various magazines of the day (Figure 2.5).

By 1833, it had become part of the Tower of London Armouries and would have been seen by many more visitors there. In January 1840, the *Penny Magazine of the Society for the Diffusion of Knowledge*, which had a circulation of 200,000 and a readership many times that number,[56] reported that the armour:

> is supposed to have belonged to one of the earliest crusaders. Could it relate its adventures, what a varied tale would it unfold [...] our thoughts revert to the time when it first saw service; its gallant wearer rises to our eyes, and although we know nothing of his history, yet, presuming him to have belonged to that numerous class of adventurers and errant knights which the pages of romance have rendered as familiar to us moderns as a troop of our own horseguard.[57]

In fact, it was later identified as of oriental origin, but as Alan Borg, the author of an article in *Country Life* chronicling this story,

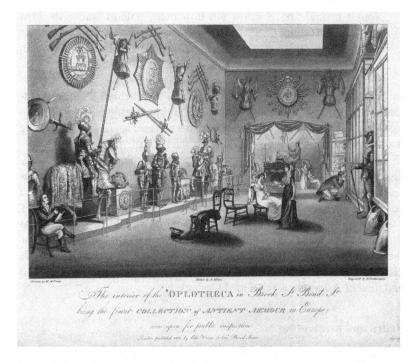

The interior of the 'OPLOTHECA in Brook St Bond St being the finest COLLECTION of ANTIENT ARMOUR in Europe now open for public inspection.

Figure 2.5 The Norman Crusader, Oplotheca, London
Source: The Trustees of the British Museum.

commented: 'The history of the Norman crusader provides an interesting sidelight on nineteenth-century romantic medievalism [...] in art [...] what is believed to be the truth is often as important [...]. The Crusader gave pleasure to many and [...] deserves a sympathetic obituary'.[58] The Tower also displayed two swords 'covered with black rust and one much eaten away', which were said to have been used by crusaders.[59]

Arms and armour associated with the crusades may indeed have been an essential requirement for an antiquarian collection, with visitors familiar with the novels of Scott; popular histories of medieval heroes, such as Richard the Lionheart; and the dramatic depictions of crusade battles staged at Astley's amphitheatre in London.[60] The poet Felicia Hemans who, if now largely forgotten, was in her time widely admired, recalled visiting Scott at Abbotsford in 1829 and being shown items from his collection:

I have the strongest love for the flash of glittering steel and Sir Walter brought out I know not how many gallant blades to show me [...] [including] one which looked as of noble race and temper as that with which Coeur de Lion severed the block of steel in Saladin's tent.[61]

In practice, the Abbotsford collection does not include a late-twelfth-century sword but, like many others at the time, Hemans's imagination would have been fuelled by reading Scott's novel, *The Talisman*, and she wrote a number of poems herself set at the time of the crusades.[62]

With arms and armour on public display and their intricacies widely discussed,[63] it is not surprising that one can also find references to crusader swords and armour in novels of the period. In 1827, the Scottish novelist Elizabeth Isabella Spence made one of her heroes boast of 'still having in his possession the steel weapon which the good knight [Bayard] had girded on in his first crusade'.[64] And the family home of the Armine family in Benjamin Disraeli's 1836 novel *Henrietta Temple* displayed the complete coat of armour worn by Ralph d'Armyn who had died at Ascalon on the Third Crusade.[65]

Relics and mementoes

A number of crusading families returned with holy relics, which they presented to their local churches and monastic foundations. A relic of the true cross, concealed on his body, is said to have ensured the safe return of the Cornish crusader Sir Roger Wallysborough from the Third Crusade and he subsequently founded the church of the Holy Cross at Grade on the Lizard Peninsula.[66] Sir Geoffrey Dutton also presented a relic of the true cross to Norton Priory in Cheshire on his return from the Fifth Crusade.[67] More unusually, an ancestor of the Irvings of Bonshaw in Dumfriesshire was said to have fought in the First Crusade and returned home with a stone from the Temple in Jerusalem that had been blessed by the Pope. Known as the crusader's stone, it was fixed to the roof of the Hall and members of the Irving clan were said to stand beneath it to receive a blessing. In fact, the stone is of local origin, but it remains another good story.[68]

Later travellers to the Holy Land also returned with their own memories and mementoes. The sword and spurs alleged to have belonged to Godfrey of Bouillon (Figure 2.6) were used in the ceremony investing new knights of the Holy Sepulchre and can still be seen on display in

Figure 2.6 Godfrey of Bouillon's Alleged Sword and Spurs, Holy Sepulchre, Jerusalem
Source: Author's photo.

Jerusalem, although they are likely to date from the thirteenth rather than the late eleventh century. Reports of the ceremony could be found in British newspapers and journals, and the popular *Illustrated London News* recorded in April 1869 that the third Marquess of Bute had been invested with the Order of the Holy Sepulchre, with the associated regalia depicted in a couple of engravings.[69] Prince Albert and Prince George, the sons of Edward, Prince of Wales, later King Edward VII, were also shown the sword and spurs by Captain Charles Conder on their visit to the Holy Land in 1882.[70]

Others brought home artefacts, such as the Syrian vase known as the Luck of Edenhall, now in the collection of the Victoria and Albert

Museum in London, and these inspired their own stories that passed into local 'folklore'.[71] The collection of the Germanisches Museum in Nuremberg also includes a small ivory replica of Godfrey of Bouillon's tomb in the Holy Sepulchre, which was brought back to Germany by a citizen of Nuremberg, Stephan Praun III, in 1585[72] and suggests a market in crusade-related mementoes.

Conclusion

The number of physical monuments and artefacts throughout Britain said to relate to the crusade have been (and still are) an important element in the shaping of the national crusade memory. Whether or not the association with the crusades can be proven in surviving sources is only part of the picture, and these monuments have both interested and inspired later generations. Thus Herbert Baker, who designed the crusade-themed First World War Memorial at Winchester College, wrote of memorable visits to the home of Lord Cobham in Kent, 'descendants of those who fought in the crusades' and during the Second World War, he was keen that church monuments remained visible because of their 'heartening influence on our spirits during the dread anxieties of the war'.[73]

Whilst modern research may challenge or dismiss claims of heroic deeds in the Holy Land, the combination of fact and fiction has produced a wealth of good stories that have been repeated in print and more recently online. As Nicholas Paul noted in his book on crusade and family memory, 'nearly every community had a "crusading ancestor" on hand to admire and contemplate'.[74] In the nineteenth century in particular, archaeological excavations (or simply finds that emerged during church improvements) reported in journals and discussed in correspondence and meetings claimed to identify new crusaders but such claims can often be traced back much further. Whilst some writers saw this as a subject for satire, it was also a source of family, local, and national pride. Moreover, those who owned or visited these monuments and artefacts did not see them in isolation. They looked at and reflected on them, drawing on knowledge of the crusades and crusaders assembled from what they had seen, heard, and read elsewhere, of tales of heroism at the siege of Acre and on the later crusades of St Louis and Prince Edward. The physical as well as the written record is therefore an important part of the jigsaw of crusade memory and legend that has been assembled in Britain over the centuries.

Notes

1 See Rosemary Sweet, *Antiquaries: The Discovery of the Past in Eighteenth-Century Britain* (London, 2004); Levi Fox, ed., *English Historical Scholarship in the Sixteenth and Seventeenth Centuries* (Oxford, 1956).

2 Richard Gough, *Sepulchral Monuments in Great Britain*, 2 vols (London, 1786–96); Charles Stothard, *The Monumental Effigies of Great Britain* (London, 1817–32).

3 Samuel. R. Meyrick, *A Critical Enquiry into Antient Armour*, 3 vols (London, 1824).

4 For a detailed discussion of how the 'myth' developed and persists, see Oliver Harris, 'Antiquarian Attitudes: Crossed Legs, Crusaders and the Evolution of an Idea', *Antiquaries Journal* 90 (2010), pp. 401–40.

5 See, in particular, Robin Griffith-Jones and David Park, eds., *The Temple Church in London: History, Architecture and Art* (Woodbridge, UK, 2017), pp. 93–134.

6 Matthew D. Wyatt and John B. Waring, *The Byzantine and Romanesque Court in the Crystal Palace* (London, 1854), pp. 46–51.

7 Jan Broadway, *'No historie so meete': Gentry Culture and the Development of Local History in Elizabethan and Early Stuart England* (Manchester, 2006), p. 195.

8 *Gentleman's Magazine* 1830 (2), pp. 399–400, 588–9. The effigy commemorates Sir John Oglander, who died in 1655. There are various stories about its origin, including that it was purchased in an antique shop in London in 1628, but in several it is described as a crusader. A smaller version in a niche above commemorates Sir John's son, George, who died in 1632. See Eric S. Hayden, *A Guide to the Church of St. Mary the Virgin, Brading, Isle of Wight* (Brading, UK, 1982), and Nikolaus Pevsner and David W. Lloyd, *Buildings of England: Hampshire and The Isle of Wight* (New Haven, CT, 2006), p. 94. See also the discussion of the crossed-legs monuments at St Clere's, Danbury, Essex, *Gentleman's Magazine*, 59 (1789), p. 496.

9 'The Crusader's tomb at Botus Fleming, Cornwall'; a letter to the editor from Thomas Quarles, *Gentleman's Magazine* (1840), p. 31.

10 Alison, 'The Crusades', p. 348.

11 *Country Life*, 22 July 1916.

12 *Brecon and Radnor Express*, 27 December 1917, p. 8. The crusader in question was Sir Grimbald de Pauncefote and the wreath was sent by his descendant, Lord Pauncefote. pp. 62, 101.

13 Oliver Harris, 'A Crusading "Captain in Khaki": Sir Thomas Brock's Monument to Charles Grant Seely at Gatcombe (Isle of Wight)', *Church Monuments* 33 (2018), 97–119. For the use of crusade imagery in First World War memorials, see Siberry, 'Memorials to Crusaders'.

14 For example, a survey of sepulchral effigies in Devon published in 1877 records some 14 crusaders. See William H. Hamilton Rogers, *The Ancient*

Sepulchral Effigies and Monumental and Memorial Sculpture of Devon (Exeter, UK, 1877).

15   Thomas Walford, *The Scientific Tourist through England, Wales and Scotland*, vol. 2 (London, 1818), p. 37, cites an example (now lost) in the ruined church at Ayot St Lawrence, Hertfordshire. Another small crossed-legs monument at Mappowder in Dorset is variously described as representing a boy crusader, a son who died whilst his father was on crusade or a heart burial. See Frederick Treves, *Highways and Byways in Dorset* (London, 1934), p. 131; Arthur Mcc, *Dorset* (London, 1939), p. 149. See also Broadway, *Gentry Culture*, p. 135.

16   Siberry, *New Crusaders*, pp. 57–8, 133.

17   See Siberry, "Nineteenth Century Perspectives of the First Crusade' in *The Experience of Crusading*, eds. Marcus Bull and Norman Housley (Cambridge, UK, 2003), p. 282. This probably refers to the Metham effigy; Gough, *Sepulchral Monuments*, vol. 1, p. 175. Etty's painting of Godfrey was exhibited in London in 1849, as noted in *Illustrated London News*, 25 August 1849, p. 135.

18   Richard Warner, *Netley Abbey: A Gothic Story* (Southampton, UK, 1795); Pevsner, *Hampshire and the Isle of Wight*, p. 348.

19   Palgrave, *Collected Historical Works*, vol. 4, p. 240. See above, pp. 25–6, 28.

20   Lord Byron, *Letters and Journals of Lord Byron with Notices of His Life*, ed. Thomas Moore (London, 1830), p. 1.

21   Washington Irving, *Abbotsford and Newstead Abbey* (London, 1835), pp. 150–1.

22   Stanley T. Williams, *The Life of Washington Irving* (Oxford, 1935), vol. 2, pp. 280–86; Brian J. Jones, *Washington Irving: An American Original* (New York, 2008), p. 204.

23   Washington Irving, *Old Christmas* (London, 1876), pp. 56, 96, 121–2, 145–9.

24   Washington Irving, *Sketchbook of Geoffrey Crayon* (London, 1881), p. 215.

25   As editor of the Philadelphia-based journal *The Analectic Magazine*, June 1814, pp. 442–56, Irving also published a review of Michaud's *Histoire*. See above, pp. 13, 17–19, 24, 28.

26   *The Chartist*, 11 (9 February 1839), p. 3. See the ODNB entry for Lord Sandon, <odnb.com>, [accessed 20 October 2020]. I am grateful to Oliver Harris for this reference and for sharing with me his detailed knowledge of church monuments.

27   Tombs of crusaders include Walter de Dunstanville in St Andrew's Church at Castle Combe in Wiltshire and Sir Roger de Carmilow, at St Mawgan in Meneage, Cornwall, said to have gone on Edward I's crusade; Sir Stephen de Haccombe, linked with the Fifth Crusade, at St Blaise, Haccombe, Devon, and Sir John Foster at St Aidan's Church, Bamburgh, Northumberland, who is said to have saved the life of Richard I at Acre. See *Find a Grave*, <www.findagrave.com>, [accessed 20 October 2020].

28   For more on Dansey, see below pp. 64–6.

29 He is not, for example, included in the most recent list of those present at the siege of Acre, in John D. Hosler, *The Siege of Acre 1189–1191* (New Haven, CT, 2018).

30 James Anderson, *A Genealogical History of the House of Yvery* (London, 1742), pp. 309–11.

31 See the ODNB entry for Joseph of Exeter, <odnb.com>, [accessed 20 October 2020].

32 Anderson, *A Genealogical History*, pp. 309–11.

33 Eleanor Porden, *Richard Coeur de Lion, or, the Third Crusade: A Poem, in Sixteen Books* (London, 1822), p. 322, l. 340. Porden's poem ran to almost 900 pages, with 150 pages of historical notes, which illustrates both the depth of her research and her access to crusade sources. See Adeline Johns-Putra, 'Eleanor Anne Porden's Coeur de Lion: History, Epic and Romance', *Women's Writing* 19 (2012), pp. 351–71.

34 The Llanarmon effigy was discussed (and illustrated) in Stephen Williams, 'Some Monumental Effigies in Wales', *Archaeologia Cambrensis*, 129 (1890), pp. 284–5. Kathryn Hurlock, *Wales and the Crusades, 1095–1291* (Cardiff, UK, 2011), p. 116, notes that there is no evidence that Gruffydd went on crusade.

35 John G. Waller, 'The Lords of Cobham, Their Monuments and Their Church', *Archaeologia Cantiana* 11 (1877), pp. 49–112.

36 Nigel Saul, *English Church Monuments in the Middle Ages: History and Representation* (Oxford, 2008), p. 228.

37 Manwaring Shurlock, *Tiles from Chertsey Abbey, Surrey, Representing Early Romance Subjects* (London, 1885). See also 'Proceedings at Meetings of the Archaeological Institute', *Archaeological Journal* 19 (1862), pp. 167–8.

38 James Cruikshank Dansey, *The English Crusaders* (London, 1850), p. 42.

39 'The Tombs of the De Broham family, with an account of some remarkable discoveries recently made in their burial place in the church of Brougham', *Archaeological Journal* 4 (1847), pp. 59–68; *Gentleman's Magazine*, 183 (1848) pp. 369–76, 618–20; 184 (1848), pp. 31–3, 138. The antiquarian Abraham Kirkmann also published an article on the Ninekirks excavation, focussing on the spur, 'On an Ivory Carving of the Thirteenth Century; with Observations on the Prick Spur', *Journal of the British Archaeological Association* 6 (1850), pp. 123–4. The ivory carving itself, a mirror case, dated from the time of Edward I and depicted 'Saracens' and crusaders, said to represent a story involving Richard the Lionheart. It was exhibited at the Ironmonger's Hall in London in 1861.

40 Chester W. New, *The Life of Henry Brougham to 1830* (Oxford, 1961), p. 1.

41 See Geoffrey T. Garratt, *Lord Brougham* (London, 1935); Mark Thomas, *A History of Brougham Hall and High Head Castle* (Chichester, UK, 1992). See also Siberry, *New Crusaders*, pp. 40–1.

42 There is a copy of the notes in the Dorset Archives, PE-SKG/AQ/1. In October 1779, workmen were also reported to have discovered a coffin containing the well-preserved body of a Knight Templar in the parish

church at Danbury in Essex. See 'Curious Leaden Coffin Found at Danbury in Essex', *Gentleman's Magazine*, 65 (1779), pp. 337–8. The church also contains two wooden effigies attributed to Knights Templar. For the historiography of the Templars in this period, see Siberry, 'Images and Perceptions of the Military Orders in Nineteenth-Century Britain', *Ordines Militares-Colloquia Torunensia Historica* 11 (2001), 197–210.

43 See *Stock Gaylard Estate*, <www.stockgaylard.com>, and *Ancient Tree Forum*, <www.ancienttreeforum.co.uk>, [accessed 20 October 2020].

44 See Revd L.B. Larking, 'On the Heart Shrine in Leybourne Church', *Archaeologia Cantiana* 5 (1863), pp. 133–94, and 7 (1868), pp. 329–41. Larking was a founding member of the Kent Archaeological Society and worked on a history of the County of Kent. See the ODNB entry for Larking, <odnb.com>, [accessed 20 October 2020], and his obituary in *Archaeologia Cantiana* 7 (1868), pp. 323–9.

45 Larking, 'On the Heart-Shrine', p. 150.

46 'History', *Leybourne Church*, <www.leybournechurch.org.uk/history>, [accessed 4 December 2020].

47 See Sally Badham, 'Divided in Death: The Iconography of English Medieval Heart and Entrails Monuments', *Church Monuments* 34 (2019), pp. 16–76. I am grateful to Sally Badham for her help on this subject.

48 For Percy's death on crusade, see Whitby Abbey, 'Cartularium Abbatiae de Whiteby', *Surtees Society* 69 (1879), p. 2, and Gerald Brenan, *A History of the House of Percy from the Earliest Times Down to the Present Century* (London, 1902), p. 8. The poem, written by William Peeris, the secretary to the Earl of Northumberland, was published in *Reprints of Rare Tracts and Imprints of Ancient Manuscripts etc. Chiefly of the History of the Northern Counties* (Newcastle, UK, 1845), pp. 19–20. There is, however, no evidence of such a heart burial.

49 Letter to *The Times*, 2 March 1925.

50 See Doherty, 'Commemorating the Past', and Roy Gilyard-Beer, 'Byland Abbey and the Grave of Roger der Mowbray', *Journal of the Yorkshire Archaeological Society* 55 (1983), pp. 61–7.

51 Revd Tony Rees, *Guidebook to St. Mary's Church, Chirk* (2004), pp. 17–19. A small figure of a knight in chainmail holding a heart in his hands at Castle Frome Church. Herefordshire is also linked with the crusades and a lead coffin found at St Cuthbert's Kirk in Edinburgh during excavations in 1773, containing an embalmed heart, was considered to have belonged to a crusader. See <https://ewh.org.uk/wp-content/uploads/2020/01/St-Cuthberts.pdf>, [accessed 9 December 2020].

52 Edith S. Hartshorne, *Enshrined Hearts of Warriors and Illustrious People* (London, 1861), p. 36.

53 Q.E.D., *The Knight's Heart: A Tale of the Crusades* (Dublin, 1895). This seems to be based on the story of Ralph de Coucy. See Revd Canon A.A.R. Gill, 'Heart Burials', *Proceedings of the Yorkshire Architectural and York Archaeological Society* 2 (1936), p. 5. See also pp. below.

54 *Goodrich Castle*, <www.bl.uk/picturing-places/articles/goodrich-castle-antiquity-and-nature-versus-thingummies>, [accessed 9 December 2020].

55 Francis Grose, *A Treatise on Ancient Armour and Weapons, Illustrated by Plates Taken from the Original Armour in the Tower of London and Other Arsenals, Museums and Cabinets* (London, 1785). Plate XXI. Grose also wrote about crossed-legs effigies linked with the crusades. See Grose, *The Antiquities of England and Wales*, vol.1 (London, 1784), pp. 145–6.

56 See Louis James, *Fiction for the Working Man, 1830–50* (Oxford, 1963), p. 15.

57 *Penny Magazine of the Society for the Diffusion of Knowledge*, 11 January 1840, p. 10. References to the crusader armour could also be found in guidebooks to London, such as Peter Cunningham, *A Handbook for London: Past and Present*, vol. 2 (London, 1849), p. 332, and *Illustrated London News*, 22 April 1848, p. 266.

58 Alan Borg, 'A Crusader in Borrowed Armour. The History of a Museum Piece', *Country Life*, 18 July 1974, pp. 168–9.

59 *Illustrated London News*, 29 March 1845, p. 201.

60 For Astley's, see Siberry, *New Crusaders*, pp. 146–7. An engraving of Richard and Saladin in combat from the production *The Crusaders of Jerusalem* was published in *Illustrated London News*, 20 May 1843, p. 343.

61 David Rothstein, 'Forming the Chivalric Subject: Felicia Hemans and the Cultural Uses of History', *Victorian Literature and Culture* 27 (1999), p. 52.

62 One such poem, titled 'The Effigies', was published in *Records of Women*, ed. Paula R. Feldman (Lexington, KY, 1999), pp. 131–2.

63 For example, in his *Encyclopaedia of Antiquities*, published in 1825, the clergyman and antiquary Thomas Fosbroke wrote about the riveted chainmail on the effigy of De L'Isle in Rampton Church, Cambridgeshire. This was later quoted in a paper on the history of English armour presented to the Liverpool Literary and Philosophical Society in January 1846. The Rampton armour also received a mention in the article on the subject in the more popular multi-volume *Penny Cyclopaedia of the Society for the Diffusion of Knowledge*.

64 Elizabeth Spence, *Dame Rebecca Berry* (London, 1827), p. 292.

65 Benjamin Disraeli, *Henrietta Temple* (London, 1836), p. 81

66 See Jo Esra, 'Cornish Crusaders and Barbary Captives: Returns and Transformations' in *Mysticism, Myth and Celtic Culture*, eds. Marion Gibson, Shelley Trower, and Gary Tregigda (London, 2012), p. 159. The story can be traced to the Tudor commonplace book of John Coleyns – BL MS Harley 2252 – and is also quoted in Dansey's list of English Crusaders, pp. 57–8. pp. 64–6. See also John P.D. Cooper, *Propaganda and the Tudor State: Political Culture in the West Country* (Oxford, 2003), p. 115. Tales of Cornish crusaders were also included in William Bottrell's *Traditions and Hearthside Stories of West Cornwall* (Penzance, UK, 1870).

67 See Chapter 4, n. 34.

68 Alan Macquarrie, *Scotland and the Crusades, 1095–1560* (Edinburgh, 1985), pp. 4–5. For stories about other Scottish crusade mementoes, see Siberry, *New Crusaders*, pp. 42–3.

69 *Illustrated London News*, 17 April 1869, p. 385. The article adds that 'the greater number of Catholic pilgrims visiting the Holy Land are invested with the insignia of the Order'.
70 Siberry, *New Crusaders*, pp. 66–7.
71 Siberry, *New Crusaders*, pp. 41–2, and <www.vam.ac.uk/>, [accessed 20 October 2020].
72 *The Germanisches Museum*, <www.gnm.de/museum>, [accessed 20 October 2020].
73 Herbert Baker, *Architecture and Personalities* (London, 1944), pp. 166, 170.
74 Paul, *To Follow In Their Footsteps*, p. 7.

3 Crusading pedigrees

The previous two chapters have considered what was available to read about the crusades, how this was debated and discussed, and the physical monuments that were believed to relate to the crusades and provided a very visible and tangible link with the past. This chapter approaches the subject of crusade memory from a different perspective, namely, the way in which families researched, celebrated, and sometimes invented a crusade ancestor and pedigree. Chapter 4 will then consider the more specific links between heraldry and the crusades.

Local and national crusaders

Recent scholarly research has focused on identifying crusaders using evidence from medieval charters and chronicles, and lists of crusaders have been published for several regions of Britain and specific crusade expeditions.[1] This, however, is only part of the story. There were many other claims of participation in the crusades, particularly as a member of Richard the Lionheart's army on the Third Crusade, which cannot be substantiated in the surviving primary sources. This does not necessarily mean that the individual concerned was not a crusader, but tales of crusading have certainly developed and been embellished over the centuries.

Validating arms and pedigrees

The desire to find and perhaps even invent a crusading ancestor is not a modern phenomenon, and the work of Nicholas Paul, Megan Cassidy-Welch, and others has underlined the early interest in identifying and remembering crusade ancestors. In Britain, the College of Arms in London, founded in 1484, maintains the official registers of heraldic coats of arms and pedigrees. It soon recognized the scope for creative genealogy and, in the sixteenth and seventeenth centuries, members of the College travelled to every county in England and Wales, regulating and registering the names and heraldic arms of those entitled to bear them and their family pedigrees.[2]

In her study of the development of local history in Elizabethan and early-Stuart England, Jan Broadway noted that the arrival of the heralds stimulated the gentry's interest in their past, and the combination of the printing press and improved literacy and education gave them the tools to 'become more than passive consumers', undertaking their own research.[3]

The original records of the Visitations are kept in the College of Arms but the Harleian Society was founded in 1869 with the objective of ensuring their publication. Organised by county, they consist of lists of the heraldry and genealogy of individual families, and the signatures of the heads of these families can often be seen attached to their respective pedigrees, underlining their ownership of the ancestral past, so to speak.[4]

It was not a straightforward undertaking, and the rigour of the enquiries made and the reliability of the information recorded varied considerably. In his article, 'Heralds, Myths and Legends', Adrian Ailes described the sensitivities and practicalities of such visits: 'It must have been virtually impossible during the early visitations, when visiting heralds met the gentry in their own homes, to question a man's ancestry (and perhaps cherished beliefs) whilst at the same time taking his money to register that ancestry and accepting his hospitality'.[5] The later proceedings became more formal and the process more professional, but testing the evidence, with its mix of oral, visual, and documentary sources, still presented real challenges. The information gathered from the Visitations, however, informed the various county histories produced by Tudor and Stuart antiquaries and on which many later histories have been based. In his study of English antiquaries, Lancaster wrote:

> Such county surveys were written primarily for readers who were themselves members of the families that were the subject matter of the books. They were the subscribers who funded the printing, they contributed plates depicting their country houses or family tombs, they gave the authors access to their 'evidences' – arms, charters, seals – and it was their ancestors whose exploits and titles were the matters of the historical narratives.[6]

The crusade ancestor

Participation in the crusades was, of course, amongst the noble ancestral deeds that families were keen to record, displaying Christian courage, devotion, and a tradition of service to the crown. And if hard evidence was not available, some families created their own ancestral narrative. For example, at the end of the sixteenth century, the Smith family, ancestors of Lord Carrington, who were anxious not to be seen as 'new gentry', concocted a link with Sir Michael Carrington, said to have been the standard bearer to Richard the Lionheart. The heralds accepted the forgery, which was recorded in the Visitation of Leicestershire, and although Dugdale had his doubts, he included the line of descent in his 1656 *Antiquities of Warwickshire* because he was apparently anxious not to offend Lord Carrington.[7] Sir Michael was subsequently included in later lists of crusaders by Jeremiah Wiffen and Dansey and quoted by authors of crusade histories, such as Charles Mills, so the story gained its own momentum.[8] In Gloucestershire, John Smyth, the seventeenth-century historian of the Berkeley family, also made sure to include a crusade ancestor to increase the family's honour: 'In the life of Harding, founder of the Berkeley family, Smyth quoted an extract from the Chronicle of Jerusalem. He did not know whether the Harding mentioned in the chronicle was the same man. However tentative, the association of the family with the crusades was worth mentioning'.[9]

Lists of crusaders

In their search for proof of crusading, families could also draw on manuscripts and then, later, published lists of crusaders.

MS Ashmole 1120 ff. 171–4

One important source for the names of English crusaders seems to have been a list of over 300 coats of arms of knights said to have been with Richard I at the siege of Acre. The document, now in the Bodleian Library as MS Ashmole 1120 ff. 171r–174v, is described as a copy made by Ralph Brooke, a member of the College of Arms, of a roll in the possession of Mr Fitzwilliams of Spotborough in Yorkshire. Hugh Fitzwilliams was MP for Peterborough and a collector of medieval manuscripts.[10] The list has the date 1563 and its contents are described as 'The names and armes of those Knightes as were wt Kinge Richard the first at the asigge of Acon or Acres; which weare copied owte of an owlde Rowle in kepynge and custoyde of Mr Fitzwilliams of Spotburghe 1563: R. Brooke als Rouge Cross'. It is, in fact, one of eleven copies of the Dering Roll, the oldest extant medieval roll of arms, which is dated c. 1275 and is now in the collection of the British Library.[11] It is unclear when and how MS Ashmole 1120 came to be described as a list of knights who fought with Richard I at the siege of Acre but this appellation appears on several other sixteenth- and seventeenth-century copics of the Dering Roll and shows again the Tudor and Stuart interest in establishing crusading ancestry.[12]

The Dering Roll has some 324 shields painted in colours on a green background, arranged in 54 rows of 6 each, most with names written above them. It is so called because it came into the possession of Sir Edward Dering, a seventeenth-century antiquary and collector of manuscripts,[13] who lived at Surrenden, Kent, and is described as a list of arms of knights predominantly from Kent and Sussex.[14] Sir Edward is known to have inserted some names and arms of fictitious Derings into the medieval rolls of arms that he possessed to enhance his family history, and he did so again here, inserting Ric fitz Dering in place of Nic. De Crioll.[15] In the nineteenth century, the Roll came into the possession of the collector Sir Thomas Phillips and it was purchased by the British Museum in 2008 from the collection of the heraldic historian Sir Anthony Wagner.

There are some significant variations in the names (both Christian names and surnames) listed in the Dering Roll and Ashmole 1120, but the detailed research carried out by Gerard Brault enables us to identify most of those listed in Ashmole 1120.[16] A number can be confirmed from original sources to have participated in the Third Crusade, but others cannot be proven as crusaders. Some errors are also repeated. For example, both list Grimbald de Pauncefote – presumably the Grimbald de Pauncefote said to have gone on crusade in the 1260s – and Roger de Leybourne, whose heart burial was discussed in the previous chapter. Neither of these was even born at the time of the Third Crusade.[17]

Ashmole 1120 was quoted as a source for two lists of crusaders published in the nineteenth century by Wiffen and Dansey and cited by later histories.[18]

Wiffen's list of English crusaders

In 1824, Jeremiah Holmes Wiffen, Librarian and Secretary to the Duke of Bedford at Woburn Abbey,[19] published a translation, in Spenserian verse, of Tasso's *Gerusalemme Liberata*. It was illustrated with a number of engravings, ran to at least four editions, and was one of a number of translations of the poem published in Britain in the nineteenth century.[20] A unique feature of Wiffen's translation, however, was that it was preceded by *A List of Such of the English Nobility and Gentry as Went on the Crusades*.

In his preface, Wiffen thanked the Duke of Newcastle and other descendants of crusading families for their help but noted that most of the names had come from his 'patient perusal of monkish annals'. He also wrote that he had consulted a manuscript at the Ashmolean Museum, which 'provided a list of those who had accompanied Richard the Lionheart on the Third Crusade and had been in the custody of the FitzWilliam family of Spotborough in Yorkshire in 1563'. This must be a reference to Ashmole 1120, and one finds therefore a repetition of names and some of the errors, such as the association of Sir Grimbald with the Third Crusade.[21]

Wiffen expressed the hope that:

> Others which may have escaped my own research, will perhaps be furnished by those who are more deeply read in county histories, in genealogy, and heraldry, and who may derive gratification from this first attempt to chronicle the names of those who, crowding from the English shores, participated in the fame of Duke Robert or Coeur de Lion, of Prince Edward, or of Salisbury.

His list numbers over 500 names and is organized chronologically, by reign, but does not give much detail on the individuals concerned, with a substantial number cited under the heading Uncertain Reigns or simply by surname. Although he states that he had read Mills's *History*, he took a rather more romanticized view of the crusades: 'Who would not willingly continue the illusion which, whether derived from the songs of our early minstrels, or the charming tale of Tasso, invests the character of the Crusader with I know not what of devotion, love and generosity'. Wiffen fortuitously managed to identify a crusading ancestor for his employer, the Duke of Bedford, namely, Roger of Barneville, who died heroically on the First Crusade. Roger's son, William, also went on the crusade, and his brother, Hugh, was said by Wiffen to have added three escallop shells to the family arms in recognition of their role on the crusade. They continue to feature in the arms of the Dukes of Bedford to the present day.[22]

The popularity of Tasso would have meant that Wiffen's list of crusaders reached quite a wide audience and copies can be found in a range of public and private libraries in Britain. It was also widely reviewed in various journals of the time. Whilst most focused on the poem and translation, some, such as the *Monthly Review*, referred to the list of crusaders, noting that 'it may minister, perhaps, to the ancestral pride of our old families'.[23]

Wiffen's subscriber list is impressive, starting with King George IV and a good selection of the British aristocracy. He would have contacted many of these families in the course of his research and they would naturally have wished to see their forbears duly acknowledged. Wiffen also knew Southey and Wordsworth, who shared his interest in the history of the crusades.[24]

Wiffen's list was reproduced by Thomas Keightley in his history of the crusades published in 1833-4, after his description of Richard I's arrival at Acre:[25]

> The first army of crusaders which England sent forth, being now landed under the command of their king, it may be gratifying to see the list of the nobles and knights of greatest note, who on this occasion "Bore the radiant red-cross shield" [...] and it will be interesting to observe what names among them still remain in the rolls of nobility, or among our territorial aristocracy. For that purpose, we subjoin the following catalogue of English crusaders.

Recognizing the strong interest amongst his readers in laying claim to such a crusade ancestor, Keightley wisely added that he was not responsible for any errors or omissions in the list, and he also queried some names, such as the inclusion of three Earls of Leicester.

Dansey: *The English Crusaders*

A much grander and more detailed list of crusaders appeared a quarter of a century later, in 1850. Its full title was *The English Crusaders; Containing an Account of All the English Knights who Formed Part of the Expeditions for the Recovery of the Holy Land. Illustrated by Three Hundred Coats of Arms and Various Embellishments, Illuminated in Gold and Colours.* The author was James Cruikshank Dansey.

Dansey was born in London in 1818, the son of Major Charles Cornwallis Dansey of the Royal Regiment of Artillery. He was educated at Christchurch, Oxford, and is listed as a member of Lincoln's Inn in London in 1838, so he may have trained as a lawyer. His only other known publication was a historical romance titled *The Persecuted, or The Days of Lorenzo dei Medici* and published in 1843.

The list of crusaders (Figure 3.1) was advertised in the journal *The Athenaeum* as 'intended to embrace interesting matter connected with

Figure 3.1 Dansey's list of crusaders
Source: Author's photo.

the crusades, from whom so many illustrious and noble families are descended',[26] and it was presumably this potential market and his own interest in history that prompted Dansey to put pen to paper. In fact, his work appeared posthumously in 1850, for he died, aged only 29, in 1847.[27]

It is a splendid and lavishly illustrated work, with coloured pages preceding each crusade, rather like a medieval illuminated manuscript. Only 100 copies were produced and there is no subscriber list, but the frequent references to noble families descended from heroic crusaders may have stimulated the market, and a copy listed in the sale catalogue of the London bookdealers, Quaritch, in 1877 noted that it contained 'valuable information for the genealogy of many of our English families'.[28]

In the Preface, Dansey took a less romanticised view of the crusades than Wiffen, noting 'those who assumed the cross were as remarkable for their enthusiastic valour as for improvidence and debauchery', but his motivation was similar, namely, 'to rescue from oblivion as many of these gallant Knights as authentic documents will furnish any account of'. He drew on similar sources and urged families who had material about crusade ancestors to share this information with him: 'The author, aware that many legends exist in private families relative to their ancestors who were at the crusades, would gladly receive any authentic communications from such parties'.

Dansey's list runs to over 1,300 names listed by expedition, with the largest number attributed to the Third Crusade. The level of detail varies considerably and, frustratingly, the names are not arranged alphabetically or even geographically. Wherever he could, however, Dansey included information about relevant events on the crusade and the contemporary descendants of the crusader in question. He also liked a good story.

Dansey cited a wide range of county histories, as well as medieval sources, but the references given in the left-hand margin lack detail and, like many others, he took as read that a crossed-legs effigy denoted participation in the crusades. Without the benefit of recent scholarship, which has shown them to be forgeries, he also drew on the Courtois charters, produced and sold in the 1840s, as French families competed for inclusion in Louis Philippe's Salles des Croisades.[29]

Dansey concluded his work with the hope that:

> having dwelt on the deeds of noble and heroic men [...] and how much they preferred glory to either pleasure or safety, their descendants may so far esteem their gallant ancestors as to approach them in all honourable endeavours and leaving mistaken enthusiasm to past ages, be ever found zealous defenders of the true faith.

This interest and pride in crusading ancestry was echoed by other local and county historians throughout Britain. One such, Alfred Edwards from Crediton in Devon, wrote in the Preface to his poem about the crusading exploits of Richard the Lionheart, published in 1878:

> Devonshire, even at such a long distance of time since these great events, can still boast of noble families whose ancestors were identified-some of them prominently so-with the early crusaders. I here especially refer to two distinguished noblemen, the Earls of Devon and Fortescue, who, both in their public and private capacities, command the admiration and esteem of all classes in this large county. And probably these Worthies of Devon are not ashamed of the fact that several of their ancestors, either from England or Normandy, fought against the Turks when they were so truly terrible; and helped to stem the advancing legions of Islamism when its power seemed almost irresistible.[30]

Edwards went on to list over 20 families whose ancestors had taken part in the Third Crusade, noting 'names that Devonshire, at least, can still boast of among her nobility'. Families also commissioned their own pedigrees, which were proudly displayed in their houses, although the evidence on which such claims were based is sometimes contradictory.

The De Lucys: An example of contradictory claims

The De Lucys of Charlecote House in Warwickshire illustrate the difficulty in validating and unravelling the various claims of crusading ancestors that have been made over the subsequent centuries. Not surprisingly, the family claimed an ancestor who had fought with Richard at Acre, a feat said to be reflected in their coat of arms.

In their survey of Kent, *Villare Cantianum*, the seventeenth-century antiquaries, John and Thomas Philpot, wrote, without further detail: 'Aymer de Lucy was with Richard I in Palestine at the siege of Accon, and in memory of some signal service there in that holy quarrel, added the cross crosslets into his paternal coat, which before was only three pisces lucii, that is pike fish'.[31] Over a hundred years later, this crusading ancestor was the subject of discussion in two popular periodicals. In 1824, a letter from a reader of the *Gentleman's Magazine* in Hereford claimed:

> Originally the arms had three luces only; but Richard the First, to reward the gallantry of Aymer de Lucy at Acon in Palestine added the crosslets. Richard and Aymer de Lucy were descendants of Fulbert de Lucy and consequently the Charlecote family must claim him as their founder, as they now bear the three luces with the crosslets.[32]

A letter published in *The Spectator* in February 1894 added:

> Few houses in England can equal Charlecote [the family house in Warwickshire now owned by the National Trust] in beauty and historical interest, but in antiquity it could not touch the ancient manor-house of the Lucys at Newington Lucy, which has only been pulled down in late years, and was the abode of Sir Aymer de Lucy, who went to the crusades and fought with such valour at the siege of Acre that King Richard allowed him to wear crosslets on his shield, which have ever since been worn on the Lucy coat of arms.[33]

The family was undoubtedly proud of this crusade association, and when in the nineteenth century George Lucy employed architects and designers to remodel his house for contemporary needs and tastes, his strong interest in family history was reflected in the interior decoration, for example, in the inclusion of heraldic stained glass by Thomas Willement.[34] Indeed, Charlecote has been described as 'saturated with heraldry', and the family coat of arms, with its crusade resonance, can be found everywhere, from carpets to furniture.[35] Lucy was also assiduous in tracing the pedigree of his ancestors and had a fine emblazoned pedigree book compiled at the College of Arms, which is now on display at Charlecote.

Once again, the crusade attribution is not easy to substantiate and there seem to have been competing claims to be the family crusader. Ashmole 1120 includes Aymer de Lucy as a member of the Third Crusade, as do Dansey and Wiffen, but he does not feature in more modern, source-based lists, although Geoffrey de Lucy, a landowner in Dorset and Devon, is substantiated as present at Acre.[36] And Nicholas Vincent's recent study of the Lucy family identifies some other possible crusaders, with no mention of Aymer.[37]

Noting that many of the relevant family papers seen by Dugdale and published in his *Antiquities of Warwickshire* were destroyed in a fire in the nineteenth century, Vincent suggests that one de Lucy ancestor, Walter Fitz Thurstan, might have been captured in the course of the Third Crusade, with his wife and son subsequently founding a small priory at Thesford dedicated to St Radegund, who was associated with the Holy Land.[38] In addition, Walter's son, Richard, is recorded as having taken the cross in the early 1240s and a kinsman, Geoffrey de Lucy of Newington, was involved in Richard of Cornwall's 1240 expedition and took the cross again in 1249.[39] To confuse things even further, in the nineteenth century, George Lucy's wife, Mary Elizabeth, compiled her own history of the family, and this refers to yet another possible crusader, Sir William, who took the cross in 1303. Yet another de Lucy, Anthony, Lord of Cockermouth and Egremont, Cumbria, also fought and died as a crusader in Lithuania in 1368 and is believed to be buried at St Bees Priory.[40] There is therefore quite a lot of evidence of de Lucy crusaders, albeit not actually the one who is celebrated in the family coat of arms.

Percy, Dukes of Northumberland, and Courtenay, Earls of Devon

The Percy and Courtenay families provide other examples of ways in which crusade pedigrees were publicly displayed. William Percy's participation in the First Crusade has already been discussed.[41] The family's pedigree roll on display at their London residence, Syon House in Middlesex, also shows a family link to Godfrey of Bouillon, through the marriage between Agnes Percy and the heir to the House of Brabant. Even more visible, at Powderham Castle, the home of the Courtenay Earls of Devon, just outside Exeter, the 10th Earl built the dining hall in medieval style, with coats of arms tracing the family history back to tenth-century France and including Sir Reginald de Courtenay, who was a member of Louis VII's army on the Second Crusade; Joscelin I, Count of Edessa; and Peter Courtenay, Latin Emperor of Constantinople. This remains a proud element of the family history, and the obituaries in *The Times* for both the 17th and 18th Earls, quoted from *Burke's Peerage*, 'the historic Frankish House of Courtenay, whose pennon waved at Crecy, Agincourt and on crusade in the Holy Land'.[42]

A petition for a crusade barony

In at least one instance, later research into family crusade history prompted a claim for reinstatement of a medieval title. The Pirie-Gordon family played a prominent part in the Order of St John, and Harry Pirie-Gordon, in particular, was fascinated by the history of the crusades.[43] In 1901, Harry's father, Edward, presented a petition to the Pretender to the French throne, who took the name Charles XI, seeking restoration of a barony in the French peerage which had been granted to his ancestor, Sir William Gordon of Castle Gordon, County Berwick, in 1270. The petition notes that Sir William, like King Louis IX, had died from disease outside Tunis in 1270. His effects had been returned to Scotland, but his successors had taken little interest in the baronial inheritance and papers had been destroyed in a fire during the Jacobite rebellion in 1746. The original petition has survived in the East Sussex archives, the county where Harry Pirie-Gordon spent his later years, but there is no surviving reply.[44] It is, however, a further example of the interest in crusade ancestry.

In Castletownshend in County Cork in Ireland, Colonel Kendall Coghill actually claimed descent from Saint Louis, himself, and his family, which included the author Edith Somerville, reflected this in a memorial window in the local church designed by Harry Clarke.[45]

Literary crusaders

Once again, the interest in crusade ancestors is echoed in the literature of the day. In *New Crusaders*, I discussed a number of examples of crusade ancestors in works of fiction by authors such as Benjamin Disraeli (particularly in his Young England trilogy) and Tennyson.[46] Further research has produced yet more examples, both of literary crusaders and writers who claimed their own crusade ancestry to underline the point.

The English writer Edward Bulwer-Lytton is said to have had an ancestor, Sir Giles Lytton who fought with Richard the Lionheart at Acre and Ascalon, and his novel, *The Caxtons a Family Picture*, published in 1849, even includes a debate about the impact of the crusades, with the main character, Austin Caxton, concluding that the crusaders had 'saved the life of Christendom'.[47] As already noted, the poet Robert Southey hoped that one of his ancestors had fought on the crusades[48] and in his poem, *The Last of the Family*, written in 1799, a servant recalls his young master who relished hearing tales of ancestral noble deeds:

> Poor Master Edward, who is now a corpse,
> When but a child, would come to me and lead me
> To the great family tree, and beg of me
> To tell him stories of his ancestors,
> Of Eustace, he that went to the Holy Land
> With Richard the Lionheart, and that Sir Henry
> Who fought at Cressy in King Edward's war.
> And then his little eyes would kindle so
> To hear of their brave deeds.[49]

Conclusion

This search for and interest in crusading ancestors, both real and imagined, is therefore another example of the way in which stories of crusading permeated the British collective memory. Whilst Britain had no equivalent of the Salles des Croisades at Versailles, which will be discussed in the next chapter, there is ample evidence of the strong desire to anchor family history in noble deeds in times past and faithful and courageous service to the crown. The crusades, and in particular, the Third Crusade, were a key element in building and celebrating a family's proud lineage against a background of contemporary social change. Since the evidence often came from the families themselves, it was difficult to find definitive proof, and once a claim was in the system, not least being recorded in the county Visitations, it could be repeated and elaborated. Whilst the romantic medievalism of the nineteenth century was a spur to the creation of such crusade ancestry, this was not a new phenomenon. Indeed, examples of the imaginative reconstruction of family ancestry can be traced to the sixteenth century, if not earlier, and each tells its own story about how and why the crusades have been remembered in Britain.

Notes

1 Kathryn Hurlock, 'Cheshire and the Crusades', *Transactions of the Historical Society of Lancashire and Cheshire*, 159 (2010), pp. 1–18, and *Wales and the Crusades*; Macquarrie, *Scotland and the Crusades*; Nicholas Orme, 'Cornwall and the Third Crusade', *Journal of the Royal Institution of Cornwall* (2005), pp. 71–7; Riley-Smith, *The First Crusaders, 1095–1131* (Cambridge, UK, 1997); James Powell, *Anatomy of a Crusade, 1213–21* (Philadelphia, 1986); Hosler, *The Siege of Acre*; Beatrice N. Siedschlag, *English Participation in the Crusades, 1150–1220* (Menasha, WI, 1939)
2 Michael Maclagan, 'Genealogy and Heraldry in the sixteenth and seventeenth centuries' in *English Historical Scholarship in the Sixteenth and Seventeenth Centuries*, ed. Levi Fox (Oxford, 1956), pp. 31–49.
3 Broadway, *Gentry Culture*, pp. 1, 153, 240.
4 See John P. Rylands, ed., 'The Visitation of the County of Dorset, 1623', *Harleian Society* 20 (1885). Indexes and guides to the Visitations were also available; for example, see Charles Bridger, *An Index to Printed Pedigrees Contained in County and Local Histories, the Heralds' Visitations and in the More Important Genealogical Collections* (London, 1867).
5 Adrian Ailes, ' "To Search the Truth": Heralds, Myths and Legends in 16th and 17th Century England and Wales' in *Genealogica et Heraldica. Proceedings of the XXVII International Congress of Genealogical and Heraldic Sciences, St Andrews, 21–26 August 2006* (St Andrews, Scotland, 2006), p. 103.
6 Charles Lancaster, *Seeing England: Antiquaries, Travellers and Naturalists* (Stroud, UK, 2008).
7 Broadway, *Gentry Culture*, pp. 123–4. See also Broadway, 'Symbolic and Self-Consciously Antiquarian: The Elizabethan and Early Stuart Gentry's Use of the Past', *Huntingdon Library Quarterly* 76 (2013), pp. 548–9.
8 p. 63. A note in the 1828 edition (p. 78n) states, 'Mr Wiffen has discovered that a Sir Michael Carrington was Richard I's standard bearer and was an ancestor of the Smiths, Lord Carrington'.
9 Broadway, *Gentry Culture*, pp. 195–6.
10 See the ODNB entry for Hugh Fitzwilliams, <odnb.com>, [accessed 20 October 2020].
11 The Dering Roll and its copies have been discussed in detail by the heraldic historian, Anthony Wagner. He suggests that the Spotborough Roll may either have been the original or a very accurate fifteenth-century copy. See Anthony Wagner, *A Catalogue of English Mediaeval Rolls of Arms* (Oxford, 1950), pp. 14–16.
12 Wagner, *Catalogue*, pp. 14–16.

13 See the ODNB entry for Edward Dering, <odnb.com>, [accessed 20 October 2020].

14 'Digitised Manuscripts, Add Roll 77720', <www.bl.uk/manuscripts/ FullDisplay.aspx?ref=Add_Roll_77720>, [accessed 20 October 2020].

15 See Wagner, *Catalogue*, p. 467; Anon, 'The Surrenden Charters', *Archaeologia Cantiana* 1 (1858), pp. 50–65. The Rous Roll, dating from c. 1483, also included some crusading additions to please the author's patron. See Mason, 'Legends', p. 29.

16 Gerard J. Brault, ed., *Rolls of Arms of Edward 1 (1272–1307)* (Woodbridge, UK, 1997), pp. 145–71. The differences may be a result of errors in copying or perhaps new information that had emerged from the Visitations and that the copyist was asked or deemed it advantageous to include.

17 See Siberry, 'A Crickhowell Crusader: The Case of the Missing Hands', *Brycheiniog* 46 (2013), pp. 101–9. For Leybourne, pp. 45–6. above.

18 Ashmole 1120 is, for example, cited as evidence that the crossed-legs effigy in Sullington Church, Sussex, was a De Covert who was present at the siege of Acre. See R.L. Hayward, *Yesterday in Sullington. The Church, the Parish and the Manor* (Sullington, UK, 1981), pp. 7–8. In 1956, A.J. Cronin, who lived in the Old Rectory in Sullington in the 1930s, published a novel titled *Crusader's Tomb.*

19 Samuel R. Pattison, ed., *The Brothers Wiffen: Memoirs and Miscellanies* (London, 1880).

20 See Lawrence, *Tasso's Art and Afterlives*, and Peter France, ed., *The Oxford Guide to Literature in English Translation* (Oxford, 2000), pp. 482–3.

21 See below, p. 101.

22 Jeremiah H. Wiffen, *Historical Memoirs of the House of Russell from the Time of the Norman Conquest* (London, 1833), vol. 1, pp. 33–43.

23 *Monthly Review* (1825), p. 318.

24 Siberry, 'Readers' Perspectives', p. 18.

25 Thomas Keightley, *The Crusaders, or Scenes, Events and Characters from the Times of the Crusades* (London, 1833–4), vol. 1, pp. 272–4.

26 *The Athenaeum* (1846) p. 467.

27 The *Gentleman's Magazine* 28 (182) 1847, pp. 182–3, recorded the death of James Cruikshank Dansey of Great Milton, Oxford, on 18 July 1847.

28 Bernard Quaritch, *A General Catalogue of Books Offered to the Public at the Affixed Price. The Supplement 1875–77* (London, 1877), p. 572. This copy was priced £6 6s and another, perhaps more used (p. 1459), at £5 5s.

29 See pp. 84–5 below.

30 Alfred Edwards, *Incidents in the Career of Coeur de Lion, Related in Verse, with Copious Notes Referring to Him and Some of the First Crusaders* (Plymouth, UK, 1878), pp. 4–5.

31 John and Phillip Philpot, *Villare Cantianum* (London, 1659), p. 248.

32 *Gentleman's Magazine*, 94 (1) (1824), p. 215. See also 92 (1) (1822), pp. 130–1; 91 (2) (1821), p. 131. Dansey also has a de Lucy on the Second Crusade.

33 *The Spectator*, 10 February 1894, p. 16.

34 Clive Wainwright, *The Romantic Interior: The British Collector at Home, 1750–80* (New Haven, CT, 1989), pp. 212–23.

35 Thomas Woodcock and John M. Robinson, *Heraldry in Historic Houses* (London, 1999), pp. 57–60.

36 Siedschlag, *English Participation*, p. 115.

37 Nicholas Vincent, *The Lucys of Charlecote: The Invention of a Warwickshire Family, 1170–1302* (Stratford-upon-Avon, UK, 2002), pp. 16, 18, 27.

38 Alice Fairfax-Lucy, *Charlecote and the Lucys* (London, 1990), p. 38, also queries whether Walter's son William might have gone on the Fifth Crusade or at least taken the cross.

39 Simon D. Lloyd, *English Society and the Crusade, 1216–1307* (Oxford, 1988), pp. 83–4.

40 I am grateful to Jessica Wolverstone at the National Trust for this reference. See Christopher J. Knusel et al., 'The Identity of the St. Bees Lady, Cumbria. An Osteobiographical Approach', *Medieval Archaeology* 54 (2010), pp. 271–311, and, in particular, pp. 292–4, 300–2, and 305–6. Knusel refers (p. 301) to a fifteenth-century roll of the Greystoke family that states that Anthony died in the Holy Land, but he attributes this as most likely due to his crusader status rather than an actual journey to the East.

41 See p. 46 above.

42 *The Times*, 24 November 1998 and 21 August 2015.

43 See Siberry, 'Variations on a Theme: Harry Pirie-Gordon and the Order of Sanctissima Sophia' in *Piety, Pugnacity and Property. Military Orders*, ed. Nicholas Morton (London, 2020), pp. 237–47.

44 East Sussex archives ASH/786.

45 See Siberry, 'Saint Louis', p. 103.

46 Siberry, *New Crusaders*, pp. 54–60.

47 Edward Bulwer-Lytton, *The Caxtons: A Family Picture* (London, 1849), vol. 2, pp. 296–7. Lytton also wrote a poem titled *The Last Crusader.*

48 See above, p. 21. Another writer, Walter Savage Landor, was said to be descended from Robert de in Lande, who had distinguished himself at the siege of Acre. Landor's ancestry was, however, debated in a letter to the editor of *The Spectator*, 25 June 1910, p. 17.

49 Southey, *Minor Poems 1823*, vol. 2, pp. 185–6.

4 The heraldic crusader

The symbols chosen for their heraldic coat of arms were another way in which families remembered and celebrated an ancestor's participation in the crusades. This provided a visible (and colourful) language to represent and display their lineage and their forebears' service and heroism in a noble cause. Heraldry was also a portable symbol that could be used not only for formal purposes but also in the decoration of houses and on show for all to see.

This chapter will first look at the role of the crusades in heraldic history and how this was discussed, and sometimes challenged, by heraldic historians, particularly in the late eighteenth and nineteenth centuries. It will then consider just a few of the many heraldic symbols linked with service on the crusades and the family stories associated with them.

The history of heraldry and the crusades

The use of devices on shields as a means of identification in battle can be traced to the twelfth century and the various elements of the complete heraldic achievement – coats of arms with their supporters, crests, and mottoes – developed over subsequent centuries.

In his chapter on heraldry in *Medieval England*, the heraldic historian Anthony Wagner wrote about how various elements combined to bring heraldry to birth:

> The developments in armour which made the individual knight ever less easily discerned save by his cognizance; the Crusade and the tournament which now brought together knights who were strangers yet rivals; the growth of feudalism and the emphasis on the knight's hereditary attachment to his lord and his land; the efflorescence of romantic chivalry and its poetic expression; and the simultaneous culmination of the decorative arts all seem to join

together to bring heraldry to birth and hereafter in one century to perfection.[1]

Wagner expanded on this history in *Heralds of England: A History of the Office and College of Arms*, published in 1967,[2] and, whilst much has been written on the history of heraldry in subsequent years, there is general agreement that the period of the crusades played a key role in the development of heraldry.

As mentioned in the previous chapter, the thirteenth and fourteenth centuries saw the production of elaborate and lavishly illustrated rolls of arms, such as the Dering Roll, that were later copied and sometimes adapted to provide evidence of crusading ancestors.[3]

In the sixteenth and seventeenth centuries, historians highlighted the role of the crusades in the development of heraldry, and the number of publications on the subject increased in the eighteenth and nineteenth centuries, together with easier access to such works through libraries and periodicals.

In 1793, the Revd James Dallaway, an antiquarian and former chaplain to the British Embassy at Constantinople, published his *Inquiries into the Origin of the Science of Heraldry in England*. He noted the key role of the crusades in the history of heraldry but also the problem with the evidence on which heraldic claims were based:

> Those chiefs, who during the holy war returned to their own country, were industrious to call forth the highest admiration of their martial exploits in the middle ranks. Ambitious of displaying banners they had borne in the sacred field, they procured every external embellishment that could render them, either more beautiful as to the execution of armorial designs, or more venerable as objects of such perilous attainment. These inclinations were encouraged by Richard I, as tending to divert the dissatisfactions of his people, from whom he was estranged; to employ the martial spirit of his nobility, and to increase that love of romantic enterprise, to which he sacrificed both his crown and life.[4]

The *Historical Anecdotes of Heraldry and Chivalry Tending to Shew the Origin of Many English and Foreign Coats of Arms, Circumstances and Customs*, published anonymously in 1795 by 'a lady' in Worcester, offered a different perspective. It is now considered to be the work of Susannah Dawson Dobson, who was on the fringes of Dr Samuel Johnson's circle and translated a key chivalric text by Saint Palaye.[5] In *Historical Anecdotes*, Dobson provided a summary of the crusading movement and the Military Orders and highlighted the role of the crusades in the development of heraldry[6]:

> Nothing seems to have contributed so much to the honour heraldry has been held in as the Crusades. The warmth with which men pursued glory in the holy war can be equaled by nothing in history. There are more families who bear arms from some meritorious achievement then, or who assumed arms on that occasion, than on any other single cause whatever. The battle of Crecy gave rise to many, but nothing can equal the crusades.[7]

Although critical of aspects of the crusades, Dobson did not really challenge the individual stories of heroism and sacrifice that had led to a grant of specific arms, but Mark Antony Lower, author of *The Curiosities of Heraldry*, published in 1845, introduced a note of caution:

> The Crusades are admitted by all modern writers to have given shape to heraldry. And although we cannot give credit to many of the traditions relating to the acquisition of armorial bearings by valorous knights on the plains of Palestine, yet there is no doubt that many of our commonest charges, such as the crescent, the escallop shell, the water-bowget etc. are derived from these chivalrous scenes.[8]

These books were reviewed in periodicals such as *The Athenaeum* and *Spectator*.[9] An advert in *The Athenaeum* declared: 'one who wishes for a copious continuous and philosophical view of heraldry and its connection with the history and manners of the Middle Ages will be amply gratified by a perusal of The Curiosities of Heraldry'.[10] And a reviewer in *The Spectator* commented:

> The Curiosities of Heraldry does not a priori seem to come so home to every family as a book where they may find the probable origin of their own name or that of some of their friends; but it will be found on perusal to be more various, comprehensive, and satisfactory [...] it will more than satisfy the expectations formed from its title, by the variety of its subjects, as well as by the agreeable manner in which they are treated, and by the author's just mixture of zeal for the science and reason to estimate its true importance.[11]

There was also debate about the accuracy of specific heraldic claims. A review of John Burke's *Genealogical and Heraldic History*[12] published in *The Athenaeum* in July 1841 noted that people were invited to send their own account of their family history and 'whatever was furnished seems to have been printed, no matter how improbable'. It also dismissed the 'idea of a crusader receiving a patent armorial ensign duly emblazoned and sealed', together with crest and motto.[13]

In his study of heraldic history, published in 1852, James Robinson Planche,[14] an expert on the history of costume, antiquary, and official Herald, was similarly critical of some of the 'absurd fancies of writers'. Whilst he recognized the importance of the crusades in heraldic history, Planche lamented: 'Had half the ingenuity and industry been exerted to discover the real origin of Armorial Insignia, which has been wasted upon inventing stories to account for them, what service might have been rendered to history, what light thrown upon genealogy and biography'.[15] He added that the crusades were particularly susceptible to such treatment:

> Another great resource for the Herald was the continual importation of exaggerated stories of the marvels witnessed and the achievements performed in the plains of Palestine. Not content with the natural motive for displaying some symbol of faith or sign of pilgrimage, some extravagant legend, some miraculous appearance, was promulgated as the cause of the assumption.[16]

Chapter 2 considered some of the debate about the attribution of physical monuments, and in Chapter 3 I discussed the ways in which families might embellish their own history. In both cases, it was not easy to challenge or dismiss such claims and the same was true of heraldry. The modern historian seeking to distinguish between fact and fiction must therefore tread with care. Nevertheless, each story tells its own tale of family pride and desire to claim a place in key events of the nation's history.

In *The Romance of Heraldry*, Wilfrid Scott-Giles, a Fellow of the Heraldry Society and an Officer of Arms, serving as Fitzalan Pursuivant Extraordinary, reflected further on the relationship between the crusades and heraldry. He was a member of The Most Noble Order of Crusaders, which was established in 1921, to promote medieval chivalric values against the background of a troubled post-First World War Britain[17] and his interest in the history of the crusades is reflected in a number of articles linking the crusades and heraldry in its journal, *The Tenth Crusade*.

Scott-Giles coined the term 'heraldic zoo' to describe the various heraldic animals that may have been inspired by participation in the crusades and gave examples of families whose heraldry laid claim to a crusading ancestor.[18] He even provided a crusading story in his spoof history of *The Wimsey Family*, chronicling the ancestors of Lord Peter Wimsey, the eponymous aristocratic detective in the novels of Dorothy L. Sayers:

> The original arms of the Wimseys are held to have been, Sable, three plates. Tradition asserts that the Baron Fulk de Wimsey (or Guimsey) encouraged King Richard I to persist in the siege of Acre, quoting to him the analogy of the patience of a cat at a mousehole; and that after the fall of the city the plates were changed into silver mice in recognition of the baron's good advice, the crest being assumed at the same time. It seems most likely, however, that the incident occurred during one of the later crusades and was transferred to an earlier date by the antiquarian enthusiasm of the family chronicler.[19]

Heraldic symbols

The phrase 'the antiquarian enthusiasm of a family chronicler' is certainly apposite when one comes to look at individual heraldic symbols and the associated family crusading tales. In his *Curiosities of Heraldry*, Lower wrote:

> It may be unnecessary to observe, that many of the anecdotes about to be related are of a very apocryphal description, referring to periods antecedent to the introduction of armorial bearings. Some of these, however, may be correct in the incidents, though incorrect in point of time; and doubtless, in many cases, the arms have been assumed in rather modern times, to commemorate the exploits of ancestors of a much earlier period; the highly prized family tradition having been confided to the safe custody of the emblazoned shield. At all events, I deliver them to the reader as I find them set down in 'myne authorities' and leave the onus probandi to the families whose honour is concerned in their perpetuation.[20]

Whilst memories and stories passed from generation to generation are not necessarily inaccurate, they can become more elaborate with the telling, and the evidential trail is therefore complex. It is, however, worth pursuing, working backwards through family and antiquarian histories to try to establish when such claims first emerged and how they have developed over subsequent centuries. And the existence of such stories and claims, even if unsubstantiated, of course tells its own story about perceptions and memories of the crusades.

The Saracen's head, the cross or crosslet, star, and a variety of birds and animals are just some of the symbols associated with the crusades.

Saracen's head

Families such as the Walpole, Earls of Orford, and Wards, Viscounts Bangor, have a Saracen's (the heraldic term) head as part of their coat of arms and have claimed that this reflects an ancestor's participation in the crusades. Tracing this to a specific crusader ancestor, however, is more difficult and, as already mentioned, the picture is further complicated by the late thirteenth- and fourteenth-century enthusiasm for tournaments in which 'Saracens' fought against Christian knights.[21]

Walpoles

The Walpole Saracen's head crest can be seen in various manifestations at the family seat, Houghton in Norfolk, but the display and pride in family history is most apparent in the house designed by the polymath Horace Walpole at Strawberry Hill in Twickenham, London. In the Library at Strawberry Hill, the ceiling 'tells the story of the Walpole family's heraldic antecedents from the time of the crusades'.[22] Two roundels depict knightly ancestors, together with the ubiquitous Saracen's head and crosslets and the armoury, a recreation in miniature of a gothic baronial hall, included weapons 'all supposed to be taken by Sir Terry Robsart in the holy wars'.[23] This carefully calculated display was probably inspired by a visit to the Palazzo Caprara in Bologna, where Walpole saw trophies of arms taken in the wars against the Turks,[24] which, as noted by the art historian George Henderson, would have been regarded as an essential element of a medievalist design: 'Strawberry Hill, for all its ecclesiastical gloomth, would not have been regarded as genuinely medieval without one or two visual reminders of the crusades. And so Walpole crammed his armoury with Near and Middle eastern junk, spears and shields of rhinoceros hide "all supposed to be taken by Sir Terry Robsart in the Holy Wars"'.[25] For some reason, Walpole seems to have confused one Robsart ancestor with another – Sir Terry with Sir John, who had taken part in wars against the Turks in the late fourteenth century.[26]

Walpole's letters reveal mixed views about the crusades. Writing to his friend, Madame du Deffand, in 1771, he was dismissive of the crusaders' enthusiasm to recover the holy places – 'la plus sotte [...]

enterprise qui pût jamais passer par la tête' [the most foolish [...] enterprise ever envisaged], but 20 years later, he commented after reading William Robertson's *Historical Disquisition*, 'I had constantly looked on the crusades as a detached isolated frenzy-you have shown that those very dark minds began to be opened, or rather reillumined, by their communication with the East'.[27]

Walpole's gothic novel, *The Castle of Otranto*, published in 1764, is also set against the backcloth of the crusades, the events described taking place sometime between 1095 and 1243, and with one of the characters, Frederic, returning from the Holy Land after being reported dead. Like other contemporaries, his Library also included a number of books relating to the crusades.[28]

In July 1783, a group of visitors to Strawberry Hill seemed to Walpole to bring the crusades very much to mind. He wrote to Lady Ossory:

> Another day the Jerninghams brought to see my house-whom do you think? -only a Luxembourg, a Lusignan, and a Montfort. I never felt myself so much in the Castle of Otranto. It sounded as if a company of noble crusaders were come to sojourn with me before they embarked for the Holy Land.[29]

Wards

The heraldry of the Viscounts Bangor, from County Down in Northern Ireland, is said to reflect the role of an ancestor, Robert Ward, at the siege of Acre on the Third Crusade. The family arms are described in some detail in Burke's *Heraldic Dictionary*, published in 1837:

> Arms-cross patonce, cinquefoils
>
> Crest – a Saracen's head couped below shoulders
>
> Supporters – dexter a knight in complete armour, on his breast a cross [...] behind him a flowing crimson robe, a cross...on the helmet a plume of feathers [...] hand resting on a drawn sword [...]. Sinister a Turkish prince vested in blue and gold, the habit reaching to the ankles, white stockings, yellow sandals and a fringe around his waist, behind him a loose brown robe of fur, on his head a white turban with black feathers, his hands chained together by a long chain.

The family motto is also *sub cruce salus* (salvation under the cross).[30]

Whilst Robert's name appears in the Ashmole list, this is not substantiated by the medieval sources, so the origins of the story and the claim remain unclear.[31] The coat of arms and attendant supporters are nevertheless proudly displayed in carpentry, plasterwork, and other media throughout the family home, Castle Ward.

There are a number of other families in Britain whose heraldry features a Saracen's head, with a purported link with the crusades, such as the Gorneys,[32] Minshulls,[33] and Duttons[34] from Gloucestershire and Cheshire, and Sir Marmaduke Darrell from Yorkshire.[35] And the symbol can be found displayed in the decoration of country houses and on various artefacts, such as china.[36]

Once again, these claims are echoed in literature. In her novel, *Daniel Deronda*, published in 1876, George Eliot's hero has an ancestor who killed three Saracens in one encounter and whose heads are included in the family coat of arms.[37]

Crosses and Crosslets

As well as the Ward, Walpole, and De Lucy families,[38] a crusading link between the use of a cross/crosslet and the crusades was made by or for T.E. Lawrence, better known as Lawrence of Arabia.

Lawrence

Lawrence was a passionate medievalist and was very knowledgeable about the crusades, having written his undergraduate thesis on crusader castles and seen many of the key sites.[39] According to some accounts, he also had a crusade ancestor, Sir Robert Lawrence of Ashton Hall in the county of Lancaster, who accompanied King Richard to Acre; was knighted for his services and granted arms of a red cross on a silver shield.[40] The American journalist Lowell Thomas, author of *With Lawrence to Arabia*, drew parallels between the medieval crusader and Lawrence's role in the Palestine campaign during the First World War:

> Among his celebrated ancestors was Sir Robert Lawrence, who accompanied Richard the Lionheart to the Holy Land seven hundred and thirty years ago and distinguished himself at the siege of Acre, just as the youthful T.E. Lawrence accompanied Allenby to the Holy Land and distinguished himself in its final deliverance.[41]

Subsequent biographers of Lawrence have expressed different views about whether it was Lawrence or Thomas who first made such a claim, but with his strong personal interest in the crusades, Lawrence does not seem to have challenged it and it is often repeated. There are, however, a number of problems with this story. Ashton Hall did not become the Lawrence home until the late thirteenth century[42] and, most importantly, Lawrence was the name taken by his mother. The original family surname was Chapman.

After his death in 1935, Lawrence was commemorated by a life-size recumbent effigy, carved by his friend, the sculptor Eric Kennington, in the church of St Martin in Wareham, Dorset. Both Kennington and Lawrence subscribed to the crossed-legs effigy crusader theory and the latter is deliberately shown as a modern crusader.[43]

Stars

Stars were another heraldic symbol associated with the crusades, often in connection with a miraculous event that turned the fortunes of a particular battle.

De Vere

Mention has already been made of John de Vere, Earl of Oxford, whose tomb at Bures in Essex displayed a Saracen's head,[44] and the family, ancestors of the present-day Dukes of St Albans and Earls of Crawford and Balcarres,[45] included in their coat of arms a five-pointed star or molet, which is reputed to commemorate the exploits of Aubrey or Alberic de Vere during the siege of Antioch on the First Crusade.

According to the sixteenth-century antiquary, John Leland, who made detailed notes of his travels through England and discussions with families, Aubrey fought at Nicaea, Antioch, and Jerusalem. During the lengthy and difficult siege of Antioch, when the Muslim army seemed likely to escape under cover of darkness, a brilliant five-pointed star appeared on de Vere's banner; the battlefield was illuminated and the crusaders were victorious:

> In the year of our Lord 1098, Corborant, Admiral to the Soudan of Persia, was fought with at Antioch, and discomforted the Christians. The Night coming on in the Chace of this Bataile, and waxing dark, the Christians being four miles from Antioche, God, willing the saufte of the christianes, shewed a white Starre or Molette of five pointes, which to every Manne's Sighte did lighte and arrest upon the standard of Albrey, then shining excessively.[46]

Wiffen, presumably drawing on this claim, states that Aubrey 'third Earl of Gisney, great Chamberlain of England, recovered by his sword the Christian banner captured at Antioch'.

No source is given for either of these miraculous events, and in his *Antiquities of Heraldry*, published in 1869, William Ellis offered a rather more prosaic explanation for the molet, linking it with Robert Malet, Aubrey's predecessor as Great Chamberlain.[47] An alternative explanation, offered in Scott-Giles's *Romance of Heraldry*, was that the star was introduced to distinguish the de Vere arms from others consisting of red and gold quarters.[48]

Nevertheless, the crusades were listed by the Victorian historian Thomas Macaulay as one of the great events of British history in which the family had participated:

> The longest and most illustrious line of nobles that England has seen, whose heads brought it honour in the fields of Hastings, Jerusalem, Runnymede, Crecy, Poitiers, Bosworth and the Court of Elizabeth where shone the 17th Earl who had won himself an honourable place among the early masters of English poetry.[49]

Birds and animal crusaders

The birds and animals said to represent participation in the crusades include swifts, because of their ability to fly long distances;[50] owls, because of their vigilance[51]; and, more surprisingly, an ass.[52]

Individual stories

There are also some more specific stories of courage in battle subsequently said to have been immortalized by heraldry. The heroism in the face of battle associated with Sir Richard de Perceval has already been mentioned[53] and there is a similar story relating to the Le Eyr/Foljambe family.

In this, the 'human leg in armour couped at the thigh quarterly and sable spurred', which is part of the heraldry of the Eyre family of Derbyshire, is said to date to an act of heroism during the Third Crusade (although another version has an earlier member of the family acting heroically at the Battle of Hastings and being rewarded by William the Conqueror). In the crusade version, Humphrey le Heyr of Bromham, Wiltshire, rescued Richard the Lionheart at the battle of Ascalon, and this act cost him his leg.[54]

A couped leg is certainly the crest of the Eyre family and a Richard le Eyr is said to have taken the cross on the Lord Edward's crusade,[55] but the origins of the story remain unclear. The much more likely explanation for a similar crest for the Foljambe family is that it was a canting device – in other words, a pun on the name.[56]

De Ros

Such 'canting' arms were popular. In his list of crusaders, Dansey also included the story of Walter de Ros, who during the Third Crusade fought his way through the Saracen army to reach the river and return to his fellow crusaders with waterskins (bougets) full of much-needed water, which Dansey gives as the origin of the water bougets in the arms of the families of Roos.[57] The family coat of arms does indeed show a bouget and is said to date from c. 1244, some 50 years after the Third Crusade. Roger of Howden, a Yorkshire neighbour, however, makes no mention of this heroic feat and just includes Walter, brother of Peter de Ros, Archdeacon of Carlisle, in the list of those from his home county who died during the siege of Acre.[58] A simpler explanation may be that the family arms were inherited from another Yorkshire family, the Trusbuts, and this is another heraldic pun.[59]

Some modern crusading echoes

There are also some more recent examples of crusade-related heraldry. The coat of arms of Sir Sidney Smith, who defended Acre against Napoleon in 1799, depicted the breach in the walls of Acre, with the standards of the Ottoman Empire and Great Britain and the motto, 'Forward Coeur de Lion'.[60] Harry Pirie-Gordon, a student of the crusades and founder of his own order of chivalry,[61] is said to have to have been present at the battle of Meggido against the Ottoman army in September 1918, advancing with the family crest – a fawn with a Turkish crescent in its mouth – on his pennant. As already noted, he also claimed a crusading ancestor who accompanied Louis IX on this second crusade and died during the siege of Tunis.

Arms as decoration: Louis Phillipe and Versailles

British families were of course not alone in claiming crusade ancestors and displaying this in their family coats of arms, and the story of the Courtois charters and the Salles des Croisades at the Palace of Versailles in France is the clearest example of this. The Salles formed part of

Louis Phillipe's scheme to celebrate the glories and triumphs of French history and, as well as a series of paintings of scenes from the crusades, the design included coats of arms of families whose ancestors were said to have taken part in the crusades.

British visitors to Versailles included Queen Victoria and the novelist Mrs Gaskell. The Queen was shown around the Salles des Croisades by Louis Philippe in August 1855 and described them as 'very handsome and quite in accordance with the times' in her journal.[62] And whilst not uncritical of the crusades themselves, the author of an article in the *Eclectic Review* in 1864, titled 'In the Footsteps of the Crusaders', commented:

> As we have walked through the gorgeous crusade rooms in Versailles, the ceilings covered with the embossements and heraldries and escutcheons of knights and heroes and vast flowing canvasses reciting the stories of their deeds [...] ah, as we walk, we say what courage, what will, what vast ideas,, what ensanguined faith [...]. So they took possession of the world for the Cross. A lie on well coloured canvass seems, somehow, so respectable and believable.[63]

Mrs Gaskell reflected on French interest in crusade ancestry in her short story, *French Life*, which was published in *Fraser's Magazine* in 1864. A visit to the castle at Chastellux prompted a discussion about the fate of families who had been represented in the Salles des Croisades:

> the company present fell to talking about the rapid disappearance of old French families within the last twenty or thirty years; during which time the value for 'long pedigrees' has greatly increased after the fifty years of comparative indifference in which they were held. [...] And now in 1864 not two-thirds of these families exist in the direct male line! Yet such has become the value afforded to these old historical titles and names that they are claimed by collateral relations, by descendants in the female line – nay, even by the pur-chasers of the lands from which the old Crusaders derived their appellations.[64]

Conclusion

What does all this signify? The examples quoted in this chapter, which are certainly not exhaustive, illustrate the diversity of heraldic symbols linked with the crusades and the imaginative stories associated with them. They also serve as further proof of the strong desire, even up to the present day, of families and places throughout Britain to claim a crusading ancestor. The romantic medievalism of the nineteenth century may have popularized and encouraged the spread of such stories, but their roots can often be found much earlier.

At another time of social change and uncertainty, in the sixteenth and seventeenth centuries, heraldry had provided the gentry with a pictorial language to display their proud lineage, some of which might be of much more recent creation. It was a means of expressing not only family pride but also continuing obligation and service. In the Preface to his 1656 *Antiquities of Warwickshire*, William Dugdale wrote that, by describing the noble actions of ancestors, he sought to 'incite the present and future ages to a virtuous imitation of them'. Such sentiments would have been understood and echoed by later generations, with service in the crusades cited in a sequence that might also include the battles of Crecy and Agincourt and support for the royalist cause during the English Civil War.

Notes

1 Anthony Wagner, 'Heraldry' in *Medieval England*, ed. Austin L. Poole (Oxford, 1958), p. 348.

2 Anthony Wagner, *Heralds of England: A History of the Office and College of Arms* (London, 1967).

3 Noel Denholm-Young, *History and Heraldry: A Study of the Historical Value of the Rolls of Arms* (London, 1965), pp. 12–13, wrote that such additions were used 'to falsify a genealogy and so to glorify a name and pander to family pride'.

4 James Dallaway, *Inquiries into the Origin of the Science of Heraldry in England* (London, 1793), p. 31.

5 See Tyerman, *Debate*, pp. 73–7.

6 Susannah Dobson, *Historical Anecdotes of Heraldry and Chivalry* (Worcester, UK, 1795), pp. 66–107, 128–72.

7 Dobson, *Historical Anecdotes*, p. 53.

8 Mark Lower, *The Curiosities of Heraldry* (London, 1845), p. 22.

9 See also George Gatfield, *Guide to Printed Books and Manuscripts Relating to English and Foreign Heraldry and Genealogy being a Classified Catalogue of Works of these Branches of Literature* (London, 1892), which illustrates the numerous publications available on this subject.

10 *The Athenaeum*, 1845, p. 1001. See also the review in *The Athenaeum*, 1871, p. 487.

11 *Spectator*, 25 January 1845, p. 15.

12 John Burke, *A Genealogical and Heraldic History of the Commoners of Great Britain and Ireland*, 4 vols (London, 1836). See also the ODNB entry for Burke, <odnb.com>, [accessed 20 October 2020].

13 *The Athenaeum*, 10 July 1841, pp. 515–16.

14 See the ODNB entry for James Planche, <odnb.com>, [accessed 20 October 2020].

15 James R. Planche, *The Pursuivant of Arms or Heraldry Founded Upon Acts* (London, 1852), p. 14.

16 Planche, *The Pursuivant*, p. 65.

17 I am grateful to Mike Horswell for this reference. For the history of The Noble Order of Crusaders, see Horswell, *Rise and Fall*, pp. 158–83.

18 C. Wilfred Scott-Giles, *The Romance of Heraldry* (London, 1929), pp. 51–65.

19 C. Wilfred Scott-Giles, *The Wimsey Family: A Fragmentary History Compiled from Correspondence with Dorothy L. Sayers* (London, 1977), p. 12.

20 Lower, *Curiosities*, p. 162.

21 See Juliet Vale, *Edward III and Chivalry*, p. 123 n. 16; Francis H. Cripps-Day, *The History of the Tournament in England and in France* (London, 1918), pp. 16–17; Loomis, 'The Pas Saladin', pp. 83–92.

22 Anna Chalcraft and Judith Viscardi, *Strawberry Hill: Horace Walpole's Gothic Castle* (London, 2011), pp. 64, 68, 70.

23 Walpole's letter to Horace Mann, in *Letters*, ed. Wilmarth S. Lewis. (New Haven, CT, 1937–83), vol. 20, p. 381.

24 Marion Harney, *Place-Making for the Imagination: Horace Walpole and Strawberry Hill* (Aldershot, UK, 2013), pp. 183–4.

25 George Henderson, *Gothic* (Harmondsworth, UK, 1967), p. 191.

26 Philip de la Motte, *The Principal Historical and Allusive Arms Borne by Families of the United Kingdom* (London, 1803), pp. 55–6, notes that Sir John took part in the crusade in Hungary against the Ottoman Turks in 1396–8.

27 Walpole, *Letters*, vol. 5, p. 6, and vol. 15, p. 211. From the letters it is also clear that Walpole knew the poem *Gerusalemme Liberata* by Tasso and the key events of the crusades.

28 Allen T. Hazen, ed., *A Catalogue of Horace Walpole's Library*, 3 vols (Oxford, 1969).

29 Walpole, *Letters*, vol. 33, p. 406.

30 Burke, *A Genealogical and Heraldic Dictionary of the Peerage and Baronetage of the British Empire*, 5th ed. (London, 1837).

31 See Siberry, *The New Crusaders*, p. 45. Enquiries with the Ward family and the Irish Genealogical Office have not provided any answer and many of the records in Dublin were destroyed in 1922. Dansey refers to Robert Warde, citing as his source a Mss in the Bibliotheque Royale in Paris but with no further details.

32 Lower, *Curiosities*, p. 168, wrote:

> The family of Newton of Bars Court in Gloucestershire, bear for their crest, on a force argent and blue, a king of the Moors armed in mail, crowned, or kneeling and delivering up his sword, in allusion to their maternal ancestor Sir Ancel Gorney's taking a Moorish king prisoner at the surrender of Acon (Acre) in the reign of Richard I.

33　Lower also described the crusading exploits of an ancestor of the Minshulls at Ascalon: The arms and crest of Minshull of Cheshire, 'azure, an estoile issuant out of a crescent, in base argent; crest an eastern warrior, kneeling on one knee, habited gules, legs and arms in mail proper; at his side a scimitar sable hilted or; on his head a turban with crescent and feather argent, presenting, with his sinister hand, a crescent of the last'. These bearings are assigned to Michael de Minshull for his valour on that occasion, but the particular nature of his exploits is not recorded.

34　Kathryn Hurlock, 'A Transformed Life? Geoffrey of Dutton, the Fifth Crusade and the Holy Cross of Norton', *Northern History* 54 (2017), pp. 15–27, looked at how the use of the Saracen's head in the arms of Sir Peter de Warburton can be linked with his grandfather Geoffrey of Dutton's participation in the Fifth Crusade and the relic of the True Cross that he brought back and gave to Norton Priory in Cheshire.

35　Dansey, *English Crusaders*, pp. 80–1, claims that Darrell acquired 'an augmentation to his arms' for his valour in Cyprus.

36　For example, the Selbys of Ightam Mote in Kent, the Prideauxs of Prideaux Place in Cornwall, and the Shirleys of Ettington, Warwickshire.

37　George Eliot, *Daniel Deronda* (London, 1973), p. 204. See also Derek Miller, 'Daniel Deronda and Allegories of Empire' in *George Eliot and Europe*, ed. John Rignall (Aldershot, UK, 1997), p. 116, and Siberry, 'Readers' Perspectives', p. 20.

38　For the De Lucys, see above pp. 67–8. Lower, p. 167 also lists the Vescis, Chetwodes, Knoles, and Villiers in this context.

39　See Malcolm D. Allen, *The Medievalism of Lawrence of Arabia* (University Park, PA, 1991); Anthony Sattin, *Young Lawrence* (London, 2014), pp. 30–1, 34, 37, 43–5, 72–4, 89–90. '

40　Burke, *Genealogical and Heraldic History,* vol. 3, p. 64.

41　Lowell Thomas, *With Lawrence in Arabia* (London, 1924), p. 10.

42　James Usher, *Notes of the Lawrence, Chase and Townley Families* (New York, 1883), p. 8.

43　See Harris, 'A Crusading "Captain in Khaki"', p. 97.

44　Geoffrey Probert, 'The Riddles of Bures Unravelled', *Essex Archaeology and History* 126 (1984–5), pp. 60–3.

45　On a visit to the Balcarres family seat, Haigh Hall, Scott was told a story of an unlucky crusader, which he recorded in the Preface to *The Betrothed*. See Siberry, *New Crusaders*, pp. 41–2.

46　*The Itinerary of John Leland, in or about the Years 1535–43*, ed. Lucy Tomlin-Smith (London, 1907), vol. 4, p. 146. See also Verity Anderson, *The De Veres of Castle Hedingham* (Lavenham, UK, 1993), p. 5. The 1995 guide to Hedingham Castle, the ancestral home in Essex, claims that Aubrey, 2nd Earl of Oxford, and Robert, his successor, also took part in the crusades, probably the Third Crusade, but the family genealogy set out in the *Complete Peerage* makes no mention of crusading, so the source of the claim remains unclear.

47　William S. Ellis, *The Antiquities of Heraldry* (London, 1869). p.100.

48 Scott-Giles, *Romance of Heraldry*, p. 64. See also Peter Coss, 'Knighthood, Heraldry and Social Exclusion in Edwardian England' in *Heraldry, Pageantry and Social Display in Medieval England*, ed. Coss and Maurice Keen (Woodbridge, UK, 2002), pp. 49–52.

49 Thomas Macaulay, *The History of England*, vol. 2 (London, 1861), p. 126.

50 Arthur Fox-Davies, *A Complete Guide to Heraldry* (London, 1961), p. 184, n. 116.

51 According to Burke, the Foxley family of Buckinghamshire associated their crest (an owl) with an ancestor's service, again on the Third Crusade:

> Richard Foxley of Foxley in the county of Bucks, accompanying Richard Couer de Lion to the Holy Land, maintained during the war a body of British bowmen (all his own tenants) in the army of that prince and during the siege of Acon defeated, by his extraordinary vigilance, a nocturnal attempt of the infidels to surprise the Christian camp. For these services, his royal master knighted him on the field of battle and caused his crest, a hand and lure, to be changed for the vigilant owl.

  A reviewer, however, dismissed this as an absurd claim using three exclamation marks. See *The Athenaeum*, 10 July 1941, p. 516. In 'The Spectre of Tappington' in Richard H. Barham's *The Ingoldsby Legends* (London, 1840), p. 476, owls are also associated with a crusader at the siege of Acre.

52 The motto of the Mainwaring family from Over Peover in Cheshire is 'Devant si je puis' [ahead if I can] and, according to one local history, the heads of the figures rest upon an ass's head and this family crest decorates the tombs and windows with the motto 'Devant si peut'. A Mainwaring, so the story goes, had his horse killed under him in the crusades; nothing daunted, he procured the only steed he could find, an ass, and exclaiming that he would not be left behind, urged the unwilling beast to the fray. See Thomas A. Coward, *Picturesque Cheshire* (London, 1926), p. 71.

53 See pp. 39–41.

54 See <www.eyrehistory.net/histeyre>, [accessed 20 October 2020]. Humphrey died in 1232 and is buried in the churchyard of St Nicholas, Bromham; see *Find a Grave*, <www.findagrave.com>, memorial ID 19082678, [accessed 20 October 2020].

55 Joseph Foster, *The Dictionary of Heraldry: Feudal Coats of Arms and Pedigrees* (London, 1989). Lloyd, Appendix 4, notes that there were several men of this name in the records for the crusades.

56 Brault, *Rolls of Arms*, vol. 2, p. 180.

57 Dansey, *English Crusaders*, pp. 87, 91.

58 Roger of Hoveden, *Gesta Regis Henrici secundi*, pp. 146–9, and *Chronica*, p. 89, ed. William Stubbs (London, 1867–71). Other members of the family also participated in the crusades. For example, William de Ros died in 1331 on the Baltic crusade, and a wall painting of a crusading St George in the church at Bradfield Combust in Suffolk commemorated Lord Roos, who died at Paphos in 1393 on his return from Jerusalem.

59 See Scott-Giles, *Romance of Heraldry,* pp. 62–3.
60 Siberry, *New Crusaders*, pp. 73–6.
61 Siberry, 'Variations on a Theme', pp. 243–4, and above p. 69.
62 Queen Victoria's Journal, Tuesday, 21 August 1855, Princess Beatrice copies 40, p. 115, <qvj.chadwyck.com/marketing/index.jsp>, [accessed 9 December 2020].
63 'The Footsteps of the Crusaders', *Eclectic Review* 7 (1864), pp. 610–12.
64 Mrs Gaskell, 'French Life', *Fraser's Magazine* 69 (1864), p. 741.

5   The absent and returning crusader

The crusades inspired numerous writers, and the idea of the departing crusader and the perils faced by his wife and family at home, as well as the uncertainty about what he would find on his return after a long absence, was particularly popular, since it offered a tempting mix of chivalry and romanticism, combined with noble service and sacrifice. It is relevant to a discussion of how the crusades have been remembered in Britain because these stories can be found in many variations and are a vivid example of how the events and consequences of the crusades captured the imagination over the centuries.

The departure

The pre-Raphaelite artist John Everett Millais was amongst those who depicted the scene as a crusader left his home and family,[1] and the *Illustrated London News* published engravings on this theme by other European artists.[2] There were also a number of songs titled 'The Crusader's Departure', with sheet music showing the departing crusader on horseback waving to his lady.[3]

For most, however, it was the absent or returning crusader that stimulated the imagination, providing all the necessary ingredients for the romantic novelist and poet, as well as authors of what is termed gothic fiction. This subject has been discussed previously but merits further consideration, looking at a broader range of sources and types of publications.

The returning crusader

In 1851, the artist and Royal Academician John Rogers Herbert, a devout Catholic who travelled to the East on several occasions in the 1840s, painted *The Crusader's Wife*, now in the collection of the Bury

Figure 5.1 John Rogers Herbert, *The Crusader's Wife*
Source: Bury Art Museum, Greater Manchester, UK.

Art Museum. It shows a female figure gazing wistfully into the distance, scanning the horizon for the sail that would mark her husband's safe return (Figure 5.1). A painting by Frederick William Pickersgill, titled *The Returning Crusader* (1846), depicted a family's welcome and relief.

The Worsley pageant

Such a scene was the inspiration for part of a historical pageant held in the grounds of Worsley Hall near Manchester, the home of the Earl of Ellesmere, in June 1914, just before the outbreak of the First World War. The pageant's script was written by the Earl of Ellesmere's librarian, Strachan Holme, and the Chairman of the Grounds Committee was the Earl's land agent, Captain Henry Vaughan Hart Davis; there was a professional pageant master, who also composed much of the music, and a cast of 1,000, many of them local schoolchildren. There were two performances, each probably attended by 10,000 people, and the event was filmed, with showings in Manchester in subsequent weeks. It must have been a splendid occasion, concluding with a great procession that was almost a mile in length.

The Worsley Pageant (Figure 5.2) depicted three scenes from history: the return of Sir Elie, Lord of Worsley, from the crusades; the Spanish

Figure 5.2 The Worsley Pageant
Source: Chetham's Library, Manchester, UK.

Armada; and the opening of the Bridgewater Canal in 1761.[4] In the first scene, Sir Elie arrives mounted on a grey charger and in full armour. In a scene more reminiscent of Merrie England and probably owing much to the novels of Walter Scott, he is greeted not only by his wife and family, but also villagers, monks, and a jester. An excerpt below from *The Song of Elie* gives a flavour of the way in which the returning crusader was depicted:

> From Paynim land comes Elie
> From clangour, strife and war,
> From battles fought right valiantly
> With many a wound and scar [...]
>
> To green and pleasant England now,
> In peace comes Elie
> To yield his sword, as he did vow
> To ever sweet Mary
>
> To dwell among his warrior freres
> In love and amity,
> And with them, thro' the rolling years,
> To seek felicity

The Sir Elie remembered in the pageant seems to be Sir Elias de Workesley, an ancestor of the Worsley family, who is said to have accompanied Duke Robert of Normandy on the First Crusade, died on his journey home, and was buried in Rhodes. It was also claimed that Elie performed such great feats of valour and strength in battle that he is sometimes described as a giant. The story can be found in nineteenth century histories of Lancashire and the *History of Wardley Hall* by Hart-Davis and Holme, published in 1908.[5]

A reviewer in *The Athenaeum* was rightly sceptical of Elie's crusading credentials:

> The historical account is well done, except for the inclusion of the inevitable 'original owner' who was possessed of the manor 'about the time of the Norman Conquest'. And who, after fighting many 'duels and combats' took part in the crusades with Robert of Normandy. It is scarcely necessary to say that we are not referred to any contemporary documents for evidence of this gallant soldier, who is credited with the alarming name of Elias Gigas. That the reader's faith in this fabulous person may be strengthened, we are told in a footnote that it is a curious act that the name Ellis is still common in the district. It does not seem to have occurred to the authors that a very few miles away is the Welsh border, where the name Ellis is still more common.[6]

But whilst there may be no evidence of such a crusader, the pageant shows that his noble deeds were clearly imprinted in local folklore and memory.

For others, recognition and welcome took more time and the return was not always a happy one. Variations on this theme can be found in poems, plays, and novels from the late eighteenth, nineteenth, and early twentieth centuries, and in family or local stories from around Britain.

Perils of absence

The artist William Bell Scott produced at least three works titled *Return from the Long Crusade* in which a rather wild-looking crusader in pilgrim dress receives a wary welcome from his wife and son.[7] A review of an exhibition of watercolours in London in 1846 described the scene depicted in George Cattermole's *The Unwelcomed Return*: 'A primeval forest, with a mounted knight gloomily taking his way across the foreground [...] a crusader coming back as crusaders were wont to do, to find his lady married to someone else, and his own drawbridge drawn up under his knightly nose'.[8] Some crusaders returned only just in time, having been given up as dead.

In 1809, the Wiltshire poet and vicar, William Lisle Bowles,[9] published a lengthy lyrical ballad titled *The Harp of Hoel*. The ballad was dedicated to the antiquarian Sir Richard Colt Hoare, whose translation of the *Itinerarium Cambriae*, Gerald of Wales's account of Archbishop Baldwin of Canterbury's tour of Wales preaching the Third Crusade, was published in 1806, and it was this work that inspired Bowles to set his poem at the time of the crusades.

The Hoel of the title is the young lord of Llandogo near Tintern Abbey in the Wye Valley, who is persuaded to leave his wife, Gwenlhian, and son to fight in the Holy Land. As a good Welshman, he plays his harp one final time and asks her to wait for him for seven summers. As the seventh summer approaches, Gwenlhian stands on a wooded hilltop. A mysterious old man appears beside her holding a horn and a mirror. In the horn she hears Hoel's voice telling her that he is coming home; in the mirror she sees him wounded after a battle. Three years later, she finally agrees to marry Hoel's friend, Einion. At the wedding party, a shabbily dressed pilgrim appears and, after playing his harp, he is identified as the long absent Hoel. Hoel and Gwenlhian are duly reunited and all ends well.[10]

British readers and travellers would also have been familiar with crusading tales and legends from French and German literature, printed in popular magazines or in cheap paper form (chapbooks) for wide circulation.[11] For example, *Theodore and Clementina*, published in 1825, was a translation of a French tale by an author who used the pseudonym Father Anselmo. In 36 pages it told the story of the crusader, Theodore, who escaped from captivity and arrived back at his castle just in time to stop the celebration of his wife's marriage with a neighbouring baron.[12] And in a Breton ballad, published in English translation in 1865, the Lord of La Fouet in Brittany returns home from crusade to find that his wife, having refused his brother's attempts to seduce her, has been left to tend the sheep. She is restored to her rightful place and the brother duly rebuked for abusing the trust placed upon him.[13]

A story of a returning crusader who returns home just in time to prevent a marriage could even be found in the American publication *The Delaware Register and Farmer's Magazine*, which interspersed useful advice on agricultural matters with stories with a moral purpose. Here, the heroine Ginevra escapes marriage to the evil Sir Leoline when the priest about to perform the ceremony reveals himself as Ralph, 'a mailed knight with the holy cross emblazoned upon his expansive breast'.[14] Not all such stories, however, ended happily.

In his Introduction to *The Betrothed*, Scott wrote:

> It was no unusual thing for a crusader, returning from the long toils of war and pilgrimage, to find his family augmented by some young offshoot, of whom the deserted maiden could give no very accurate account, or perhaps to find his marriage-bed filled, and that, instead of becoming nurse to an old man, his household dame had preferred being the lady love of a young one.[15]

And in his novel, *Waverley*, published in 1814, Wilibert of Waverley returns from the Holy Land to find that his betrothed had 'wedded the hero who had protected her from insult and oppression during his absence'.[16]

Such circumstances offered full scope to the romantic literary imagination. Popular poets, such as Felicia Hemans and Letitia Landon (known as LEL), wrote of crusaders who came home to find their wives remarried or even dead,[17] and in Amelia Opie's 'The Warrior's Return', Sir Walter arrives home to find that his son had followed him to the East and been killed in a dispute over the spoils of victory.[18] These female poets were writing against the background of the Peninsular War and it has been suggested that the adoption of a medieval theme was a way of disguising their opposition to the war, the casualties it had inflicted, and its impact on those left behind.[19]

As another variation on the theme, the crusader Sir Leoline, in the poem *The Crusader's Return* by Eliza Cobbold, returns to find his castle laid waste, his mother in hiding, and his father dead.[20] And in William Wordsworth's early drama, *The Borderers*, first written in 1796–9 but not published until 1842, Baron Herbert returns from the crusade,[21] blind and frail, to find that his land and wealth have been confiscated.[22]

Such unhappy endings were echoed in tales from elsewhere in Europe, available in translation. In Friedrich Schiller's 1797 ballad, Knight Toggenburg, the crusader returns to find that his beloved has entered a convent and spends the rest of his life in a 'hovel' waiting for a glimpse of her face from the cloister window. A number of artists produced illustrations of the lonely crusader, and some composers set the story to music, including a ballad by Schubert.[23] The poet Henry Wadsworth Longfellow even visited Toggenburg in 1835 and was inspired to write his own version of the tale.[24] The popularity of such stories is again reflected in Thackeray's choice of a returning crusader as the subject for his burlesque, *A Legend of the Rhine*, published in 1853.

Gothic tales

Imaginations roamed freely, as illustrated by the very popular novel *The Black Monk; or, The Secret of the Grey Turret*, which was serialized in 1843–4 in one of the many so-called penny dreadfuls published weekly. This combined the historical and gothic literary traditions.[25] Its author was James Malcolm Rymer – whose varied career included a patent for engraved furniture castors – and it was a reworking of Scott's *Ivanhoe*. The hero is Sir Rupert Brandon who, predictably, had fought beside Richard the Lionheart on the Third Crusade. He had left England believing that his wife had died in childbirth and, in his absence, a sinister Black Monk, the Jesuit Morgatini, arrives at the castle, which has been left in the hands of Rupert's brother, Eldred, and his late wife's sister, Agatha Weave. Plots abound and for many months there is no news of the absent crusader, but in due course a knight, Sir Kenneth Hay, arrives at the castle to carry out Sir Rupert's business. A group of crusaders follow and are eventually revealed to be King Richard and Rupert. They of course defeat Morgatini and his conspirators and all ends happily, with Rupert's children discovered safe, having been looked after by the Wizard of the Red Cave.[26]

Marital complications

Absence on the crusades could also produce other marital complications. In the Introduction to *The Betrothed*, Scott referred to the story of Count Ernst of Gleichen, said to have been captured on the Emperor Frederick II's crusade and freed through the intervention of his captor's daughter. In gratitude, he promised to marry her and obtained papal permission to take a second wife. His first wife is said to have accepted the situation in relief at his safe return, and the trio lived happily thereafter. They can certainly be seen depicted together in murals in the city hall in Erfurt and on their tombstone in Erfurt Cathedral. The tale also inspired a short opera by Schubert, *Der Graf von Gleichen*.[27]

The story was mentioned in Kenelm Digby's chivalric text, *The Broad Stone of* Honour,[28] and his account inspired his friend Wordsworth to write a poem, *The Armenian Lady's Love*, in 1829–30 in which the now Armenian princess enables a Count to escape from captivity and returns to Germany with him and is welcomed by his wife. The poem concludes:

> Mute memento of that union
> In a Saxon church survives,
> Where a cross-legged knight lies sculptured
> As between two wedded wives.
> Figures with armorial signs of race and birth
> And the vain rank the pilgrims bore while yet on earth.[29]

Grieving at home

There were also stories of those who grieved and worried back home. The waterfall, Aira Force, on the western side of Ullswater in the Lake District is associated with the tale of Emma, whose betrothed, Sir Eglamore, had left on crusade. Believing him to be dead, she fell into a sleepwalking trance and when he unexpectedly returned and she was awakened, she slipped and fell to her death. Broken-hearted, Eglamore became a hermit and lived in a cave near the waterfall. Wordsworth was amongst those inspired by the story, composing his poem *The Somnambulist* in 1828.[30]

These stories appear in unlikely places. Thus, in 1898, the *Montgomery and Radnor Baptist Visitor*, a monthly periodical for members of the Baptist community in Mid Wales, featured the story of Agnes, who was pursued by another whilst her favoured suitor, Hugo, was away. She took comfort from 'a favourite old love romance' that featured the Lady Elaine and the crusader knight, Brittmart. In this, Brittmart is told by an eastern magician that she has been unfaithful, and Elaine hears from his rival for her hand in marriage that Brittmart is dead. Both Elaine and Agnes, however, remain steadfast and the latter resolves 'to reject all other offers and still to cherish the hope that she might see her beloved again'.[31] This is a suitably moral tale that illustrates how this became a familiar plotline.

The crusader, of course, might also return badly wounded or even dying. And in 1837, the American artist Thomas Cole painted two landscapes, titled *The Departure* and *The Return*. The former showed a band of crusaders setting out in the early summer light, led by their lord on a white horse. The latter at eventide depicted a smaller group carrying the body of their dying lord, with his rider-less horse trailing behind. Both are now in the National Gallery of Art in Washington.[32]

Crusader ghosts

As a further variation on the theme, there are a number of stories about crusader ghosts. In Cornwall, Sir Ralph (or Reginald) Blanchminster near Bude, is said to have returned from Edward I's crusade to find that his wife had remarried. He then spent the rest of his life living in the castle grounds and, after his death, was said to haunt the castle moat.[33] The much-damaged effigy of a crossed-legs knight can still be seen in nearby Stratton Church, and a history of the church comments:

> And, even if, as must be admitted, no evidence has been produced, or perhaps is ever likely to be produced, to support the crusader tradition, still it must be remembered that a certain weight must be allowed to the tradition itself, for these voices from the past are seldom without some basis of fact.[34]

The tale certainly features in a number of county histories and inspired the Revd Stephen Hawker, a collector of Cornish tales, to write a poem titled 'Sir Ralph de Blanchminster of Bien Amie'.[35]

Ghosts also appear in some other poems and novels. One of Scott's earliest works was a translation of the German ballad *William and Leonore* by Gottfried August Burger, published in 1774. The original tale was set in the aftermath of the Prussian victory at the battle of Prague in 1757, but Scott chose to place the action in a crusading context, with the title 'William and Helen'. At the beginning of the poem, Helen is anxiously awaiting news of William's return. He duly appears and she leaves with him on horseback as midnight strikes. He takes her not to be married, however, but to his grave, which swallows both horse and riders.[36]

In Ann Radcliffe's popular novel, *The Mysteries of Udolpho*, published in 1794, the ghost of an English crusader, Sir Bevys of Lancaster, who has been murdered on his way home from the Holy Land, asks a French baron to arrange for his body to receive a proper burial.[37] A variation on this tale also formed the plot of Radcliffe's novel *Gaston de Blondeville*, published posthumously in 1826. Here, a visitor to the court of King Henry III at Kenilworth Castle seeks justice for his kinsman, Reginald de Folville, a Knight of St John, who had been murdered by robbers in the forest of Arden on his return from the Holy Land. The events are depicted in a pageant performed before the king that includes a ghostly apparition of the murdered crusader and takes place in the Great Hall decorated with tapestries of scenes from the Third Crusade.[38]

The imprisoned crusader

One reason for a lengthy absence was imprisonment, and this seems to have inspired a number of poets, including William Morris.[39] It also created its own set of stories and local legends.[40]

The Irish knight Bertram de Verdun is believed to have prepared for this eventuality by dedicating the house of the cruciferi at Dundalk to St Leonard, the patron saint of captives and prisoners of war, before his departure on crusade.[41] Others, however, are said to have called upon the saint after the event. One such tale is depicted in a mid-nineteenth-century stained-glass window at Wroxall Abbey (until recently a hotel) in Warwickshire. It tells the story of Hugh de Hatton in nine lights or scenes. Hugh is first shown leaving for the crusade and embracing his wife and children; then being taken prisoner in battle and confined in prison for seven years. After praying for his release, he receives a vision of St Leonard, the patron saint of prisoners, and is miraculously transported, still in his chains, to Wroxall, where he is found by one of his herdsmen. At first, his wife fails to recognize him, but she does so eventually when he shows her his half of a ring.[42] Whatever the circumstances, in gratitude for his release, Hatton gave 3,000 acres of land to found the Benedictine priory of Wroxall, dedicated to St Leonard and including the broken ring and fetters amongst its possessions.[43] The date of the priory's foundation is usually given as c. 1135, so it is not clear which crusade was involved, but, although William Dugdale expressed his doubts in his county history, the moral tale of piety and faithfulness is part of local legend. When the banker and mill owner, James Dugdale, built his new house near the ruined priory in 1866–8, he chose the story for the window, made by stained-glass designer Thomas Drury.[44]

St Leonard also features in a similar story from Yorkshire. According to the tale, a local knight, Sir Leonard of Ryseby, went on crusade; was captured; was miraculously set free; returned home just in time to prevent his wife's second marriage; but died soon afterwards and was made a saint. He appeared, still in his chains and shackles, near Thrybergh, at a place later marked by a cross known as Sir Leonard's cross. The returning crusader was apparently depicted in a window in the church until at least the seventeenth century, and visitors could also see his shackles.[45] The story also inspired a poem by James Ross in 1817 and follow-up correspondence in local newspapers; although later historians have again not been able to identify the crusader, the story seems to have been popular in the area.[46] It even re-emerges in a First World War memorial window at Apethorpe in Northamptonshire, where St Leonard of Reresby is paired with St Leonard of Limoges. The designer Christopher Whall gave as his reason for this choice of subject the escape from captivity of France and England through their ultimate victory.[47]

There might also be consequences for the crusader's wife back home. For example, Lady Sybil, the wife of Sir Grimbald de Paunceforte, is said to have cut off her right hand to send as ransom for the release of her crusading husband, and her effigy in the parish church in Crickhowell is indeed handless. There is no evidence that Grimbald went on crusade, and wear and tear over the centuries is the more prosaic explanation for the state of Lady Sybil's effigy.[48] However, whilst analysis of the sources may prove that such events never occurred, the stories remain in the popular imagination.

The jealous crusader

Another variant was the returning crusader who imagined, without real evidence, that his wife had been unfaithful during his absence. In 1779, the artist Henry Fuseli painted *Ezzelin and Meduna* (now in the Sir John Soane Museum in London), which depicted the invented story of a crusader who killed his wife on grounds of infidelity during his absence. The painting was admired by Lord Byron and engraved by a number of later artists. And at Alvercote in Warwickshire, there is a story of William Burdet, who returned from crusade and wrongly suspected that his wife had been unfaithful with his steward. Burdet is said to have cut off her hands as she held them up in supplicating posture and she died of her injuries.[49] In another version of this tale, attributed to Dugdale's *History of Warwickshire* by Dansey, he stabbed her in the heart:

> William Burdet, Kt., served in Palestine 1192; he then assumed, in addition to his armorial bearing, a crescent and a star, as a badge of his services as a crusader. On his return from the Holy Land, William Burdet committed an act which was the source of deep remorse. His steward, during his absence, attempted the chastity of his lady; and having experienced a most indignant repulse, resolved, in order to conceal his treachery, to accuse her of infidelity on his master's return. This accusation so enraged Sir William that upon his wife's approaching to embrace him, he stabbed her to the heart. Her innocence was shortly afterwards discovered.

Sir William is said to have founded the priory of Alvercote in expiation.[50]

An even more grisly tale comes in South Wales and concerns the Berkerolles of St Athans. Sir William (or, in some versions, Sir Jasper) Berkerolles is said to have gone on the Second Crusade and on his return accused his wife, Lady Clare, of having been unfaithful. He initially locked her in a room to starve, but servants secretly supplied her with food. He then buried her up to her neck in a field near the castle and all were forbidden to provide her with food or drink. Her sister used to visit her, and the dew on her dress gave Lady Clare brief relief, but she died after 10 days. Once again, the accusation was proved false and Sir William was overcome with grief and guilt. The ghost of Lady Clare's sister, called the Lady in White, is still said to be seen gathering dew in the fields.[51]

Conclusion

It is not surprising that the mix of noble knightly endeavour and the consequences for those left behind inspired so many and varied tales, drawing both on local history and legend and stories from other countries. The origins of individual tales are now almost impossible to trace but the range of authors, from Scott and Wordsworth to gothic novelists and contributors to popular magazines, underlines the extent to which the crusades captured the romantic imagination. In some cases, the screen of medieval history may also have been a convenient vehicle of protest in time of war and reflecting the anxiety felt by those left behind. Such stories were echoed across Europe and the Atlantic. They are not simply literary curiosities. They matter because, in understanding and analysing the ways in which the crusades have been remembered, there is no rigid line between popular fiction and historical fact. Such tales, appearing in many forms and media, therefore form part of the complex jigsaw of crusading memory discussed in previous chapters.

Notes

1 Siberry, 'The Crusader's Departure and Return: A Much Later Perspective', *Gendering the Crusades*, eds. Susan B. Edgington and Sarah Lambert (Cardiff, 2001), pp. 177–8. Millais's paintings were exhibited publicly and are now in collections such as the Ashmolean Museum in Oxford. They probably inspired another Pre-Raphaelite artist, Joanna Boyce Wells, to paint *The Departure: An Episode of the Child's Crusade*, which was exhibited at the Royal Academy in London in 1859.

2 For example, *The Parting* by the Austrian artist Wilhelm Koller, *Illustrated London News*, 9 May 1874, p. 438.

3 See Siberry, 'The Crusader's Departure', pp. 186–8.

4 *Redress of the Past*, <www.historicalpageant.ac.uk>, [accessed 20 October 2020]. Chetham's Library in Manchester has copies of the pageant souvenir, the vocal music, and various postcards and photographs. I am grateful to Fergus Wilde, the librarian, for his help with enquiries.

5 Henry V. Hart-Davis and Strachan Holme, *History of Wardley Hall, Lancashire and its Owners in Bygone Days* (Manchester, 1908), pp. 10–11; Cyrus Redding, *An Illustrated History of the County of Lancaster* (London, 1842), p. 88; John Harland and Thomas T. Wilkinson, *Lancashire Legends, Traditions, Pageants, and Sports* (London, 1882), p. 78.

6 *The Athenaeum*, 1908 (2), p. 605.

7 Siberry, 'The Crusader's Departure', p. 179.

8 *Illustrated London News,* 2 May 1846, p. 280.

9 See the ODNB entry for William Bowles, <odnb.com>, [accessed 20 October 2020]. He later became chaplain to the Prince Regent.

10 *The Poetical Works of William Lisle Bowles*, ed. George Gilfillan (Edinburgh, 1855), vol. 1, pp. 201–15. I am grateful to Dr Mary-Ann Constantine for drawing my attention to this poem.

11 For example, *Blackwood's Lady's Magazine* (1837), pp. 65–70, published the story 'The Crusader's Oath', heard on a tour of Germany, in which a departing crusader binds his hapless daughter to marry against her wishes if he returns safely.

12 'Gothic Fiction', *Adam Matthew Digital*, <www.ampltd.co.uk/digital_guides/gothic_fiction/Introduction.aspx>, [accessed 7 December 2020].

13 'The Crusader's Wife' in *Ballads and Songs of Brittany*, ed. Tom Taylor (London, 1865), pp. 71–2. This poem was illustrated by the artist James Joseph Tissot. See Siberry, 'The Crusader's Departure', pp. 178–9, 189.

14 'The Crusader. A Tale of the Eleventh Century', *The Delaware Register and Farmer's Magazine* (1), pp. 464–70.

15 Scott, *The Betrothed*, p. x. See also, Siberry, *New Crusaders*, pp. 116–17.

16 Walter Scott, *Waverley* (Edinburgh, 1814), pp. 37–8.

17 Siberry, 'The Crusader's Departure', pp. 181–4. In *The Crusader* (1842), the Canadian artist, James Edward Freeman, depicted a returned crusader kneeling at the tomb of his bride who had died in his absence.

18 Amelia Opie, *Collected Works*, eds. Shelley King and John B. Pierce (Oxford, 2009), pp. 149–53.

19 See Clare B. Saunders, 'Louise Stuart Costello and Women's War Poetry', *The Wordsworth Circle* 43 (2012), p. 179.

20 Eliza Cobbold, *Six Narrative Poems* (London, 1787).

21 William Wordsworth, *The Borderers*, ed. Robert Osborn (Ithaca, 1982), pp. 86–9. The crusade is not specified but the action that blinded Herbert is set in Antioch, and Wordsworth may have conflated the siege of Antioch on the First Crusade and its loss to the Mamluks in 1268. He is known to have read Fuller's *Historie of the Holy Warre*.

22 In a similar vein, in Clara Reeve's *The Old English Baron*, pp. ix–xiii (1777, repr. Oxford, 2008), Sir Philip Harclay returns from the East to find that his friend, Lord Lovel, is dead and his heir dispossessed.

23 Franz Schubert, *Ritter Toggenburg* (1816).

24 Friedrich von Schiller, 'Knight Toggenburg', in *Poems of Places*, vol. 16, <www.bartelby.com>, [accessed 20 October 2020]. In another popular German tale, a returning crusader sells his soul to the Devil to secure his wife's release from the clutches of a local robber chief. See 'The Devil's Ladder' in Charles Knox, *Traditions of Western Germany. The Rhine and its Legends* (London, 1841), pp. 163–76, and Joseph Snowe, *The Rhine, Legends, Traditions, History, from Cologne to Mainz*, vol. 2, 267–83 (London, 1839). See also Knox, 'The Chapel on the Stromberg' and 'The Knight of the Boppard', pp. 1–23, 151–62.

25 James, *Fiction for the Working Man*, pp. 83–4, 88.

26 James M. Rymer, *The Black Monk, or The Secret of the Grey Turret*, ed. Curt Herr (Richmond, VA, 2014). See also James, *Fiction for the Working Man*, pp. 41–2, 98–9, 103, 113, 172.

27 John J. Weisert, 'Graf von Gliechen "Redivivus"', *Monatshefte* (40) 1948, pp. 465–70.

28 Digby, *The Broad Stone of Honour*, pp. 69–70. For Digby's influence, see Girouard, *Return to Camelot*, pp. 55–66.

29 William Wordsworth, *Last Poems 1821–50*, ed. Jared Curtis (Ithaca, NY, 1999), pp. 173–80, 446–8. In a poem by Alfred W. Cole, published in *Bentley's Miscellany* in 1851, the abandoned lady follows Sir Raymond of Altondale back to Scotland and stabs him in revenge for his betrayal.

30 William Wordsworth, *Sonnet Series and Itinerary Poems, 1820–45*. ed. Geoffrey Jackson (Ithaca, NY, 2004), pp. 570–1, 612–19, 653–4.

31 *Montgomery and Radnor Baptist Visitor*, 3 June 1898, p. 15, <www.newspapers.library.wales>, [accessed 20 October 2020].

32 <www.nga.gov/collection/art-object-page.166439.html>, [accessed 20 October 2020]. Cole's work in turn influenced the artist George Inness, who painted *The March of the Crusaders* in 1850, now in the Fruitlands Museum, Harvard University.

33 *Castles and Manor Houses around the World*, <www.castlesandmanorhouses.com>, [accessed 20 October 2020].

34 Frederick Bone, *The Story of Stratton Church* (Plymouth, UK, 1919), p. 20.

35 Revd Stephen R. Hawker, *The Cornish Ballads With Other Poems* (Oxford, 1869), p. 38.

36 Walter Scott, *The Chase and William and Helen: Two Ballads*, translated from the German of Gottfried Augustus Burger (Edinburgh, 1796). For the popularity of this grisly tale, see Shirley N. Garner, 'Gothic Fictions: Romantic Writing in Britain' in *Cambridge Companion to Gothic Fiction*, ed. Jerrold E. Hoyle (Cambridge, 2002), p. 103. Scott also wrote a ballad, *The Fire King*, about the imprisoned crusader Count Albert and his lady Rosalie, which was depicted again by the artist Fuseli.

37 Ann Radcliffe, *The Mysteries of Udolpho* (London, 1794), pp. 552–7.

38 Ann Radcliffe, *Gaston de Blondeville* (London, 1833, repr. Oxford, 1970), vol. 1, pp. 117–23; vol. 2, pp. 71–82. See also Angela Wright, *Britain, France and the Gothic, 1764–1820* (Cambridge, 2013), pp. 108–9, 113.

39 In *A Good Knight in Prison*, Sir Guy spends 10 years in prison in the East before returning home. William Morris, *The Early Romances of William Morris in Prose and Verse* (London, 1913), pp. 78–9, and Lionel Stevenson, *The Pre-Raphaelite Poets* (Chapel Hill, NC, 1972), p. 12.

40 The Vernon family of Hanbury Hall in Worcestershire, for example, claim Adjutor Vernon, who is said to have spent 20 years as a prisoner after the First Crusade and returned home after the intercession of the Virgin Mary. See Cassidy-Welch, *Remembering the Crusades*, p. 137.

41 Hurlock, *Britain, Ireland and the Crusades, c. 1000–1300* (Basingstoke, UK, 2013), p. 122. Orderic Vitalis recorded that Bohemond of Antioch had invoked St Leonard when imprisoned, and there are numerous other such stories. See Mason, 'Legends', p. 30.

42 A tale of an absent crusader, associated with Kilchurn Castle, on Loch Awe in Scotland, was also related to visitors and published in their travel accounts. See Nigel Leask, *Stepping Westward* (Oxford, 2020), p. 202. It inspired yet another poem by Wordsworth – *Address to Kilchurn Castle*.

43 'Houses of Benedictine nuns, Priory of Wroxall', <www.british-history.ac.uk/vch/warks/vol2/pp70-73>, [accessed 20 October 2020]. Dansey links Hugh with the Third Crusade, citing as his source 'the old chroniclers'. A similar story was associated with Sir John Attwood of Wolverley Court near Kidderminster, although the tomb of the supposed crusader is dated to the mid-fourteenth century. See Broadway, *Gentry Culture*, p. 140

44 Nikolaus Pevsner and Alexandra Wedgwood, *Buildings of England: Warwickshire* (London, 1966), pp. 484–5.

45 *The Memoirs of Sir John Reresby (1634–89) Written by Himself*, ed. James J. Cartwright (London, 1875).

46 James Ross, *Wild Warblings* (Rotherham, UK, 1817), p. 16.

47 Siberry, 'Memorials to Crusaders'.

48 Siberry, 'A Crickhowell Crusader', pp. 101–9.

49 An effigy of a handless lady at Seckington, Warwickshire, has become associated with this story. See Harris, 'Beards: True and False', *Church Monuments* 28 (2013), pp. 124–32.

50 William Dugdale, *Antiquities of Warwickshire* (London, 1656), p. 613. A villainous reeve who murders a crusader's wife who refuses to marry him is also associated with Stapleton Castle in Herefordshire. See Margaret N. Turner, *Joseph Murray Ince 1806–59: The Painter of Presteigne* (Almeley, UK, 2006), p. 19.

51 See Alvin Nicholas, *Supernatural Wales* (Gloucestershire, UK, 2013), p. 59, and Jane Pugh, *Welsh Ghostly Encounters* (Llanwrst, UK, 1990), p. 80. The church at St Athans has a crossed-legs effigy of Sir Roger de Berkerolles (d. 1351) and his wife, Lady Katherine, but the origin of the ghostly tale remains unclear.

Conclusion

This study has drawn on a growing body of research and publications, as well as a wide and rich vein of previously untapped sources, to show how and why the crusades have become part of Britain's collective history and cultural memory bank. It provides further insight into the ways in which this memory has been informed, shaped, recorded, and received over the centuries, in a wide variety of media. Whilst illustrative examples have been cited from other centuries and countries, its focus has been nineteenth century Britain, when nostalgia for an age of chivalry and romantic medievalism combined with a growing interest in and engagement with the countries in which the crusades to the East had been fought. Family, local, regional, and national pride in stories of the crusaders' sacrifice and heroism were also consistent themes. The local and personal informed the national memory and vice versa.

The first step in such an analysis has been to consider what was available to read on the crusades and how such material was read and disseminated. Whilst access to primary sources and histories of the expeditions would initially have been limited, developments in printing technology meant that a wide range of relevant publications became accessible through libraries and booksellers. In some cases, individual records of reading have survived, in letters, diaries, and footnotes. Interest in and debate on the subject can also be seen in the plethora of periodicals and popular magazines that were published on a weekly, monthly, or quarterly basis to satisfy an eager readership. These included detailed articles, essays, and reviews about the crusades targeted at different audiences and opinion groups, many of which expected the reader to have some previous knowledge of the subject. Illustrations of scenes from the crusades were also widely reproduced as engravings and will have imprinted their own version of events on the eye and mind. In some instances, one can identify the stimulus of recent events or a religious motivation. In others it was a more general interest in the impact and influence of a movement that was regarded by some as bringing long-term benefits to the West, and by others as the very opposite. The memory of the crusades has been shaped by much more than just the written word. As discussed in the second chapter, the growing interest in archaeology and history led to discoveries of physical artefacts linked with (or said to be linked with) the crusades and in some cases skeletons of crusaders themselves. Indeed, it seems that almost every county in Britain can draw on some physical relic of crusading. The myth of the crossed-legs crusader has proved difficult to dispel, even in the twenty-first century, but whether true or not, it has been the source of many stories of local crusaders. Debates about individual discoveries and conclusions reached a wider audience through the letters columns of newspapers and periodicals. Once again, images played their part, not least in the numerous engravings of the effigies in the recently restored Temple Church in London, and visitors to the Great Exhibition in 1851 would also have seen the imposing statues of Richard the Lionheart and Godfrey of Bouillon.

Moreover, crusading was part of the rich tapestry of family history. Tales of noble and heroic crusading ancestors passed from generation to generation, and whilst the best of the early antiquarians sought documentary proof, they often had to rely on family memory and tradition. This desire to identify and celebrate a crusade ancestor can be traced to the time of the crusades themselves, but the sixteenth century provided an important 'bridge' and the foundations laid and claims made then persisted through subsequent centuries. They were recorded in early printed county histories and antiquarian journals and still appear in modern guidebooks and webpages. Such stories of heroism and sacrifice, particularly as members of the Third Crusade, certainly developed with the telling, but this mix of fact and fiction is of interest in its own right. This market for identifying family crusaders was served (and fuelled) by manuscript and then published lists of crusaders. The desire to claim and, if necessary, invent a crusading pedigree can also be seen in fiction and its appeal to satirists of contemporary manners and affectations.

The development of heraldry ran in parallel with the crusades, and Chapter 4 looked at how this was discussed in some detail in heraldic histories. Various heraldic symbols have been linked with specific crusading exploits, particularly on the Third Crusade. The same problems arise when one tries to trace such claims to primary sources, but again the trail of transmission tells its own story. Whilst Britain did not have its own version of Louis Philippe's *Salles des Croisades* at Versailles, heraldry was a pictorial and easy way to display and celebrate noble lineage in the aristocratic castle and gentry manor house, and many examples of this can still be seen today.

Issues of disputed inheritance and financial and family problems caused by lengthy absence, death, or injury can be found in the medieval records. It is not therefore surprising that tales of absent and returning crusaders appear in many media, from paintings to novels, short stories, and poems. The final chapter showed how much this subject appealed to all types of authors, from the romantic poet to the gothic novelist and the contributors to the so-called penny dreadful magazines. It had all the ingredients to stimulate the literary imagination and met the seemingly endless appetite for tales of thwarted romance and heroic sacrifice. The story of an abandoned crusader's wife heard on travels to the Rhineland or devoured in a popular magazine therefore needs to be added to the mix and understanding of how the crusades were received and have been remembered in Britain.

The mental jigsaw and memory map of the crusades in Britain have been formed by many strands of written record, imagery, and storytelling – personal, local, and national. As the nineteenth century progressed, the known events of the crusades and the stories of the key individuals involved were increasingly available to readers through a wide range of publications, and the views expressed in debate and print suggest real and informed interest in the subject. Britain is also rich in physical artefacts associated with the crusades, even if some of these have now been proved by modern scholarship to be of very different origin. At a family, local, regional, and national level, the crusades provided the necessary elements of a good story – national duty, sacrifice in a noble and religious cause, danger, and an exotic location. Tales of crusaders embellished the family's honour and might need to be invented if the appropriate facts were not easily available. The tapestry of memory often blurred, either intentionally or simply through the passing of time, the line between known fact and imagined events and the exact demarcation can now be difficult to establish. The interplay between fact and fiction can also be seen in the wide variety of fictional tales of crusaders available to nineteenth-century readers. It was therefore no accident that Scott chose the crusades as the background to several novels and poems, and their imprint continues to influence the memory of the crusades and crusaders to the present day.

Bibliography

Primary

Manuscripts

Bodleian Library: MS Ashmole 1120 ff. 171r-174v.
Bristol Library Society Registers. Bristol Central Library.
'Edward Pirie-Gordon petition', *Ashburnham Family Archive, East Sussex Archives ASH/786*.
'Stock Gaylard papers', *Dorset Archives PE-SKG/AQ/1*.

Printed material

Alison, Archibald. 'The Crusades'. *Blackwood's Magazine* 59 (1846), pp. 475–92.
——— *Essays Political, Historical and Miscellaneous*. Edinburgh: W. Blackwood, 1850.
Anderson, James. *A Genealogical History of the House of Ivery*. London, 1741.
Anon. 'The Surrenden Charters'. *Archaeologia Cantiana* 1 (1858), pp. 50–65.
Barham, Richard H. 'The Spectre of Tappington'. In *The Ingoldsby Legends*. London: Richard Bentley, 1840.
Bergerac, Berenice de. *The Oxford Pageant of Victory 1919*. Oxford: Vincent Works, 1919.
Berington, Joseph. *The Literary History of the Middle Ages*. London: David Bogue, 1846.
Bottrell, William. *Traditions and Hearthside Stories of West Cornwall*. Penzance, UK: W. Cornish, 1870.
Bowles, William Lisle. *The Poetical Works of William Lisle Bowles*. ed. George Gilfillan. Edinburgh: James Nichol, 1855.
Brault, Gerard B. ed. *Rolls of Arms Edward I (1272–1307)*. Woodbridge, UK: Boydell, 1997.
Bridger, Charles. *An Index to Printed Pedigrees Contained in County and Local Histories, the Heralds' Visitations and in the More Important Genealogical Collections*. London: J.R. Smith, 1867.
British Controversialist, and Literary Magazine. London: Houlton and Sons, 1852 and 1870.

Bulwer-Lytton, Edward. *The Caxtons: A Family Picture*. 3 vols. London: Blackwood, 1849.

Burke, John. *A Genealogical and Heraldic History of the Commoners of Great Britain and Ireland Enjoying Territorial Possessions of High Rank, but Uninvested with Heritable Honours*. 4 vols. London: Colburn, 1836.

———— *A Genealogical and Heraldic Dictionary of the Peerage and Baronetage of the British Empire*. 5th ed. London: Colburn, 1937.

Byron, Lord George. *Letters and Journals of Lord Byron with Notices of His Life*. ed. Thomas Moore. 2 vols. London: J. and J. Harper, 1830.

Cobbold, Eliza. *Six Narrative Poems*. London: C. Dilly, 1787.

Coleridge, Samuel. *Essays on His Times in 'The Morning Post' and 'The Courier'*. ed. David V. Erdman. Princeton, NJ: Princeton University Press, 1978.

Cunningham, Peter. *A Handbook for London: Past and Present*. London: John Murray, 1849.

Dallaway, James. *Inquiries into the Origin of the Science of Heraldry in England*. London: Cadell, 1793.

Damiani, F. 'Memoir on the Vicissitudes of the Principality of Antioch, during the Crusades'. *Archaeologia* 15 (1806), pp. 234–63.

Dansey, James Cruikshank. *The English Crusaders Containing an Account of All the English Knights Who Formed Part of the Expeditions for the Recovery of the Holy Land. Illustrated by Three Hundred Coats of Arms and Various Embellishments, Illuminated in Gold and Colours*. London: Dickinson and Co., 1850.

de la Motte, Philip. *The Principal Historical and Allusive Arms Borne by Families of the United Kingdom*. London: J. Nichols and Son, 1803.

Digby, Kenelm. *The Broad Stone of Honour, The True Sense and Practice of Chivalry: Tancredus*. London: Rivington, 1828.

Disraeli, Benjamin. *Henrietta Temple*. London: Routledge, 1836.

Dobson, Susannah. *Historical Anecdotes of Heraldry and Chivalry*. Worcester, UK: Holl and Brandish, 1795.

Dugdale, William. *Antiquities of Warwickshire*. London: Thomas Warren, 1656.

Edwards, Alfred. *Incidents in the Career of Coeur de Lion, Related in Verse, with Copious Notes Referring to Him and Some of the First Crusaders*. Plymouth, UK: Brendon, 1878.

Eliot, George. *Daniel Deronda*. London: Penguin, 1973.

Ellis, William S. *The Antiquities of Heraldry*. London: John Russell Smith, 1869.

Fosbroke, Thomas. *Encyclopaedia of Antiquities*. London: John Nichols and Son, 1825.

Gaskell, Mrs. 'French Life'. *Fraser's Magazine* 69 (1864), pp. 739–52.

Gibbon, Edward. *The Life and Letters of Edward Gibbon with His History of the Crusades*. London: Warne, 1880.

Gough, Richard. *Sepulchral Monuments in Great Britain*. 2 vols. London: J. Nichol, 1786–96.

Grose, Francis. *A Treatise on Ancient Armour and Weapons, Illustrated by Plates Taken from the Original Armour in the Tower of London and Other Arsenals, Museums and Cabinets.* London: S. Hooper, 1786–9.

Guizot, Francois. *History of Civilization in Europe.* Oxford: OUP, 1837.

Hamilton Rogers, William H. *The Ancient Sepulchral Effigies and Monumental and Memorial Sculpture of Devon.* Exeter, UK, 1877.

Hart-Davis, Henry V. and Strachan Holme. *History of Wardley Hall, Lancashire and its Owners in Bygone Days.* Manchester, UK: Sheratt and Hughes, 1908.

Hartshorne, Edith S. *Enshrined Hearts of Warriors and Illustrious People.* London: Robert Hardwicke, 1861.

Hawker, Revd. Stephen. *The Cornish Ballads with Other Poems.* Oxford: J. Parker, 1869.

Hemans, Felicia. 'The Effigies'. In *Records of Women.* ed. Paula Feldman. Lexington: University Press of Kentucky, 1999, pp. 131–2.

Irving, Washington. *Abbotsford and Newstead.* London: Bohn, 1835.

────── *Sketchbook of Geoffrey Crayon.* London: Ward Lock, 1861.

────── *Old Christmas.* London: Macmillan, 1876.

Jacob, Samuel. *History of the Ottoman Empire, Including a Survey of the Greek Empire and the Crusades.* London: Richard Griffin and Company, 1854.

Keightley, Thomas. *The Crusaders, or Scenes, Events and Characters from the Times of the Crusades.* 2 vols. London: John W. Parker, 1833–4.

Kirkmann, Abraham. 'On an Ivory Carving of the Thirteenth Century; with Observations on the Prick Spur'. *Journal of the British Archaeological Association* 6 (1850), pp. 123–4.

Knight, Charles. *Half Hours of English History.* London: F. Warne, 1851.

Knightley of Fawsley, Lady. *Politics and Society: The Journals of Lady Knightley of Fawsley 1885–1913.* ed. Peter Gordon. Northampton, UK: Northamptonshire Record Society, 1999.

Knox, Charles. *Traditions of Western Germany: The Rhine and its Legends.* London, 1841.

Lardner, Dionysius. ed. *Cabinet Cyclopaedia.* 133 vols. London: Longman, 1830–49.

Larking, Lambert B. 'On the Heart-Shrine in Leybourne Church'. *Archaeologia Cantiana* 5 (1863), pp. 133–94.

Lawrance, Hannah. 'The Crusades as Described by Crusaders'. *British Quarterly Review* 18 (1853), pp. 63–101.

Leland, John. *The Itinerary of John Leland in or about the Years 1535–43.* ed. Lucy Tomlin-Smith. London: G. Bell, 1907–10.

Lower, Mark A. *The Curiosities of Heraldry.* London: J.R. Smith, 1845.

Macaulay, Thomas. *The History of England.* 5 vols. London: Longman, 1849–61.

Mackay, Charles. *Memoirs of Extraordinary Popular Delusions.* London: Bentley, 1841.

Mackintosh, James. *History of England.* London: Longman, Brown, Green and Longman, 1830.

Mackintosh, Robert J. ed. *Memoirs of the Life of Sir James Mackintosh.* 2 vols. London: Edward Moxon, 1836.

Meyrick, Samuel. *A Critical Inquiry into Antient Armour as it Existed in Europe but in Particular in England from the Norman Conquest to the Reign of Charles II with a Glossary of Military Terms of the Middle Ages.* 3 vols. London: Robert Jennings, 1824.

Michaud, Joseph Francois. *Histoire des croisades illustree de 100 grand compositions par Gustave Dore.* Paris, 1877.

Mills, Charles. *History of the Crusades.* London: Longman, Hurst, Rees, Orme and Brown, 1820.

Morris, William. *The Early Romances in Prose and Verse.* London: Dent, 1913.

Opie, Amelia. *Collected Works.* ed. Shelley King and John B. Pierce. Oxford: OUP, 2009.

Owenson, Sydney (Lady Morgan). *The Novice of Saint Dominick.* London: Richard Phillips, 1806.

Palgrave, Francis. *The Collected Historical Works of Sir Francis Palgrave.* 4 vols. Cambridge: CUP, 1921.

Pattison, Samuel. ed. *The Brothers Wiffen: Memoirs and Miscellanies.* London: Hodder and Stoughton, 1880.

Philpot, John and Thomas Philpot. *Villare Cantianum.* London: Lynn, 1659.

Planche, James R. *Souvenir of the Bal Costume given by Queen Victoria at Buckingham Palace, May 12 1842.* London, 1843.

——— *The Pursuivant of Arms, or Heraldry Founded Upon Acts.* London: W.N. Wright, 1852.

Porden, Eleanor, *Richard Coeur de Lion, or, The Third Crusade: A Poem, in Sixteen Books.* 2 vols. London: G. and W.B. Whitaker, 1822.

'Proceedings at Meetings of the Archaeological Institute'. *Archaeological Journal* 19 (1862), pp. 167–8.

Q.E.D. *The Knight's Heart: A Tale of the Crusades.* Dublin, 1895.

Quaritch, Bernard. *A General Catalogue of Books Offered to the Public at the Affixed Price. The Supplement 1875–77.* London: Quaritch, 1877.

Radcliffe, Ann. *The Mysteries of Udolpho.* London: G.G. and J. Robinson, 1794.

——— *Gaston de Blondeville.* London: Henry Colburn, 1826, repr. Oxford: OUP, 1970.

Redding, Cyrus. *An Illustrated History of the County of Lancaster.* London: How and Parsons, 1842.

Reeve, Clara. *The Old English Baron.* 1777, repr. Oxford: OUP, 2008.

Reresby, Sir John. *Memoirs Written by Himself.* ed. James J. Cartwright. London: Longman, 1875.

Roger of Hoveden. *Chronica.* ed. William Stubbs. London: Longman, 1867–71.

——— *Gesta Regis Henrici secundi.* ed. William Stubbs. London: Longman, 1867–71.

Ross, James. *Wild Warblings.* Rotherham, UK: T. Crookes, 1817.

Russell, William. *The History of Modern Europe.* London: Jones & Co., 1814.

Rylands, John P. 'The Visitation of the County of Dorset, 1623'. *Harleian Society* 20 (1885).

Rymer, James M. *The Black Monk; or, the Secret of the Grey Turret.* ed. Curt Herr. Richmond, VA: Valancourt, 2014.

Saladin, 'The Crusades'. *Secular Review* (1884), pp. 3–14.

———— *The Crusades: Their Reality and Romance.* London: W. Stewart & Co., 1885.

Schiller, Friedrich von. *Poems of Places.* www.bartelby.com. [Accessed 20 October 2020].

Scott, Walter. *The Chase and William and Helen: Two Ballads.* Edinburgh: Manners and Miller, 1796.

———— *Waverley.* Edinburgh: Constable, 1814.

———— *St. Ronan's Well.* Edinburgh: Archibald Constable, 1824 and Edinburgh University Press, 1995.

———— *Tales of the Crusaders.* Edinburgh: Constable, 1825 and Edinburgh University Press, 2009.

———— *Tales of a Grandfather.* 3 vols. Edinburgh: Cadell, 1831.

Shurlock, Manwaring. *Tiles from Chertsey Abbey, Surrey, Representing Early Romance Subjects.* London: W. Griggs, 1885.

Snowe, Joseph. *The Rhine, Legends, Traditions, History, from Cologne to Mainz.* London: Wesley, 1839.

Southey, Robert. *The Life of Wesley and the Rise and Progress of Methodism.* 2 vols. London: Longman, 1820.

———— *Catalogue of the Valuable Library of the Late Robert Southey.* London: Compton & Ritchie, 1844.

———— *The Collected Letters of Robert Southey.* eds. Lynda Pratt, Tim Fulford, and Ian Packer. www.romantic-circles.org. [Accessed 20 October 2020].

Spence, Elizabeth. *Dame Rebecca Berry.* London: Longman, 1827.

Stothard, Charles. *The Monumental Effigies of Great Britain.* London: 1817–32.

'The Crusader's Wife'. *Ballads and Songs of Brittany.* ed. Tom Taylor. London: Macmillan, 1865.

The Debater's Handbook of Controversial Topics. London: Houlston and Wright, 1868.

'The Footsteps of the Crusaders'. *Eclectic Review* 7 (1864), pp. 610–12.

Theodore and Clementina. London: Hodgson and Co., 1825.

Usher, James. *Notes of the Lawrence, Chase and Townley Families.* New York, 1883.

Wagner, Anthony. *A Catalogue of English Medieval Rolls of Arms.* Oxford: OUP, 1950.

Walford, Thomas. *The Scientific Tourist through England, Wales and Scotland.* vol. 2. London: J. Booth, 1818.

Walpole, Horace. *Letters.* ed. Wilmarth S. Lewis. New Haven, CT: Yale University Press, 1937–83.

———— *A Catalogue of Horace Walpole's Library.* ed. Allen T. Hazen. Oxford: OUP, 1969.

Warner, Richard. *Netley Abbey: A Gothic Story.* Southampton, UK: William Lane, 1795.

Watt, Robert. *Bibliotheca or a General Index to British and Foreign Literature.* 4 vols. Edinburgh: A. Constable, 1824.

Whitby Abbey. 'Cartularium Abbatiae de Whiteby'. *Surtees Society* 69 (1879), p. 2.

Wiffen, Jeremiah H. *The Jerusalem Delivered of Torquato Tasso.* Edinburgh: Hurst, Robinson and Constable, 1824.

———— *Historical Memoirs of the House of Russell from the Time of the Norman Conquest.* London: Longman, 1833.

Willement, Thomas. *Album of Designs and Illustrations for Presentation to Lord Abergavenny,* 1818.

Wordsworth, William. *The Borderers.* ed. Robert Osborn. Ithaca, NY: Cornell University Press, 1982.

———— *Last Poems 1821–50.* ed. Jared Curtis. Ithaca, NY: Cornell University Press, 1999.

———— *Sonnet Series and Itinerary Poems, 1820–45.* ed. Geoffrey Jackson. Ithaca, NY: Cornell University Press, 2004.

Secondary

Websites

Allen, Trevor. 'WWII Martin B-26 Marauder Crews'. *B26.com.* www.b26.com/historian/martin_b26_marauder.htm. [Accessed 20 October 2020].

Ancient Tree Forum. www.ancienttreeforum.co.uk. [Accessed 4 December 2020].

Bartelby. www.bartelby.com. [Accessed 20 October 2020].

Bury Art Museum. buryartmuseum.co.uk. [Accessed 9 December 2020].

Castles and Manor Houses around the World. www.castlesandmanorhouses.com. [Accessed 20 October 2020].

'Collected Letters of Robert Southey'. eds. Lynda Pratt, Tim Fulford, and Ian Packer. www.romantic-circles.org. [Accessed 20 October 2020].

Crediton Parish Church. 'The Buller Memorial'. www.creditonparishchurch.org.uk/history/the-buller-memorial. [Accessed 20 October 2020].

'Digitised Manuscripts, Add Roll 77720'. www.bl.uk/manuscripts/FullDisplay.aspx?ref=Add_Roll_77720. [Accessed 20 October 2020].

Find a Grave. www.findagrave.com. [Accessed 20 October 2020].

Gage, Deborah. 'A Short History of Fawsley, Northants'. *FIRLE.* www.firle.com/a-short-history-of-fawsley-northamptonshire. [Accessed 20 October 2020].

Germanisches Museum. www.gnm.de/museum. [Accessed 20 October 2020].

Goodrich Castle. www.bl.uk/picturing-places/articles/goodrich-castle-antiquity-and-nature-versus-thingummies. [Accessed 20 October 2020].

'Gothic Fiction: Rare Printed Works from the Sadleir-Black Collection of Gothic Fiction at the Alderman Library, University of Virginia'. *Adam Matthew Digital.* www.ampltd.co.uk/digital_guides/gothic_fiction/Introduction.aspx. [Accessed 7 December 2020].

'History'. *Leybourne Church.* www.leybournechurch.org.uk/history. [Accessed 4 December 2020].

History of the Eyre Surname. www.eyrehistory.net/histeyre. [Accessed 20 October 2020].

Montgomery and Radnor Baptist Visitor. www.newspapers.library.wales. [Accessed 20 October 2020].

National Gallery of Art: The Departure. www.nga.gov/collection/art-object-page.166439.html. [Accessed 20 October 2020].

Oxford Dictionary of National Biography (ODNB). www.odnb.com. [Accessed 20 October 2020].

Queen Victoria's Journal. www.queenvictoriasjournals.org. [Accessed 20 October 2020].

Rothley Parish Council. www.rothleyparishcouncil.org.uk. [Accessed 20 October 2020].

St Bees Priory. www.stbees.org.uk. [Accessed 20 October 2020].

St Cuthbert's Kirkyard. https://ewh.org.uk/wp-content/uploads/2020/01/St-Cuthberts.pdf. [Accessed 9 December 2020].

Stock Gaylard Estate. www.stockgaylard.com. [Accessed 20 October 2020].

The Redress of the Past: Historical Pageants in Britain. www.historicalpageants.ac.uk. [Accessed 20 October 2020].

Victoria & Albert Museum. www.vam.ac.uk. [Accessed 20 October 2020].

Books and articles

Abulafia, David. 'Invented Italians in the Courtois Charters'. In *Crusade and Settlement*. ed. Peter Edbury. Cardiff, UK: University College Cardiff Press, 1985, pp. 134–43.

Ailes, Adrian. '"To Search the Truth": Heralds, Myths and Legends in 16th and 17th Century England and Wales'. In *Genealogica et heraldica. Proceedings of the XXVII International Congress of Genealogical and Heraldic Sciences, St. Andrews, 21–26 August 2006*. St. Andrews, Scotland: The Heraldry Society of Scotland and the Scottish Genealogy Society, 2006, pp. 95–106.

Allen, Malcolm T. *The Medievalism of Lawrence of Arabia.* University Park: Pennsylvania State University Press, 1991.

Anderson, Verity. *The De Veres of Castle Hedingham.* Lavenham, UK: Dalton, 1993.

Andrews, Stuart. 'Southey, Coleridge and Islam'. *Wordsworth Circle* 46 (2015), pp. 105–16.

Badham, Sally. 'Divided in Death: The Iconography of English Medieval Heart and Entrails Monuments'. *Church Monuments* 34 (2019), pp. 16–76.

Baker, Herbert. *Architecture and Personalities.* London: Country Life, 1944.

Bale, Anthony. ed. *The Cambridge Companion to the Literature of the Crusades.* Cambridge: CUP, 2019.

Bone, Frederick. *The Story of Stratton Church.* Plymouth, UK: W. Brendon, 1919.

Bonnett, Alastair. 'The Agnostic Saladin'. *History Today* (2013), pp. 47–52.

Borg, Alan. 'A Crusader in Borrowed Armour. The History of a Museum Piece'. *Country Life* 18 July 1974, pp. 168–9.

Brenan, Gerald. *The History of the House of Percy from the Earliest Times Down to the Present Century.* London: Freemantle, 1902.

Brewster, David. ed. *Edinburgh Encyclopaedia.* Edinburgh: Blackwood, 1830.

Broadway, Jan. *'"No historie so meete": Gentry Culture and the Development of Local History in Elizabethan and Early Stuart England.* Manchester, UK: MUP, 2006.

——— 'Symbolic and Self-Consciously Antiquarian: The Elizabethan and Early Stuart Gentry's Use of the Past'. *Huntingdon Library Quarterly* 76 (2013), pp. 541–58.

Brown, Ian. *The Edinburgh History of the Book in Scotland.* 4 vols. Edinburgh: Edinburgh University Press, 2007–12.

Cassidy-Welch, Megan. ed. *Remembering the Crusades and Crusading.* Abingdon, UK: Routledge, 2017;

——— and Anne E. Lester. 'Memory and Interpretation: New Approaches to the Study of the Crusades'. *Journal of Medieval History* 40 (2014), pp. 225–37.

Chalcraft, Anna and Judith Viscardi. *Strawberry Hill: Horace Walpole's Gothic Castle.* London: Francis Lincoln, 2011.

Chancellor, Valerie E. *History for their Masters: Opinion in British History Textbooks, 1800–1914.* Bath, UK: Adams and Dart, 1970.

Constable, Giles. 'The Historiography of the Crusades'. In *The Crusades from the Perspective of Byzantium and the Muslim World.* eds. Angeliki E. Laiou and Roy Parviz Mottahedeh. Washington, DC: Dumbarton Oaks, 2001, pp. 1–21.

Cooper, John P.D. *Propaganda and the Tudor State: Political Culture in the West Country.* Oxford: OUP, 2003.

Coss, Peter. 'Knighthood, Heraldry and Social Exclusion in Edwardian England'. In *Heraldry, Pageantry and Social Display in Medieval England.* eds. Peter Coss and Maurice Keen. Woodbridge, UK: Boydell Press, 2002.

Coward, Thomas A. *Picturesque Cheshire.* London: Methuen, 1926.

Cripps-Day, Francis H. *The History of the Tournament in England and in France.* London: B. Quaritch, 1918.

Crossley, Ceri. *French Historians and Romanticism. Thierry, Guizot, the Saint Simonians, Quinet and Michelet.* London: Routledge, 1993.

Denholm-Young, Noel. *History and Heraldry. A Study of the Historical Value of the Rolls of Arms.* Oxford: OUP, 1965.

Dickens, Bruce. 'The Nine Unworthies'. In *Medieval Literature and Civilization: Studies in Memory of G.N. Garmonsway.* eds. Derek A. Pearsall and Ronald A. Waldron. London: Athlone Press, 1969, pp. 228–33.

Doherty, James. 'Commemorating the Past in Late Medieval England: The Worksop Priory Tabula'. *English Historical Review,* 2020.

Ellenblum, Ronnie. *Crusader Castles and Modern Histories.* Cambridge: CUP, 2007.

Elliott, Andrew B.R. *Medievalism, Politics and Mass Media.* Woodbridge, UK: Boydell, 2017.

Esra, Jo. 'Cornish Crusaders and Barbary Captives: Returns and Transformations'. In *Mysticism, Myth and Celtic Culture*. eds. Marion Gibson, Shelley Trower and Gary Tregigda. London: Routledge, 2012.

Fairfax-Lucy, Alice. *Charlecote and the Lucys*. London: Gollancz, 1990.

Foster, Joseph. *The Dictionary of Heraldry: Feudal Coats of Arms and Pedigrees*. London: Bracken, 1989.

Fox, Levi. ed. *English Historical Scholarship in the Sixteenth and Seventeenth Centuries*. Oxford: OUP, 1956.

Fox-Davies, Arthur. *A Complete Guide to Heraldry*. London: Nelson, 1961.

France, Peter. *The Oxford Guide to Literature in English Translation*. Oxford: OUP, 2000.

Freeman, Jennifer M. *W.D. Caroe: His Architectural Achievement*. Manchester, UK: MUP, 1990.

Garner, Shirley N. 'Gothic Fictions: Romantic Writing in Britain'. In *Cambridge Companion to Gothic Fiction*. ed. Jerrold E. Hoyle. Cambridge: CUP, 2002.

Garratt, Geoffrey T. *Lord Brougham*. London: Macmillan, 1935.

Gatfield, George. *Guide to Printed Books and Manuscripts Relating to English and Foreign Heraldry and Genealogy being a Classified Catalogue of Works of these Branches of Literature*. London: Mitchell and Hughes, 1892.

Gill, Canon A.A.R. Revd. 'Heart Burials'. *Proceedings of the Yorkshire Architectural and York Archaeological Society* 2 (1936), pp. 5.

Gilyard-Beer, Roy. 'Byland Abbey and the Grave of Roger de Mowbray'. *Journal of the Yorkshire Archaeological Society* 55 (1983), pp. 61–7.

Girouard, Mark. *The Return to Camelot. Chivalry and the English Gentleman*. New Haven, CT: Yale University Press, 1981.

Godwin, Edward and Stephanie Godwin, *Warrior Bard: The Life of William Morris* London: George G. Harrap & Co., 1947.

Goebel, Stefan. *The Great War and Medieval Memory: War, Remembrance and Medievalism in Britain and Germany, 1914–1940*. Cambridge: CUP, 2017.

Griffith-Jones, Robin and David Park. eds. *The Temple Church in London: History, Architecture and Art*. Woodbridge, UK: Boydell, 2017.

Guard, Timothy. *Chivalry, Kingship and Crusade: The English Experience in the Fourteenth Century*. Woodbridge, UK: Boydell, 2013.

Hamilton, Bernard. 'An Anglican View of the Crusades: Thomas Fuller's *The Historie of the Holy Warre*'. *Studies in Church History* 49 (2013), pp. 121–31.

Hapgood, Kathleen. 'The Friends to Literature: Bristol Library Society 1772–1894'. *Avon Local History and Archaeology Publication* 7 (2011).

Harland, John and Thomas T. Wilkinson. *Lancashire Legends, Traditions, Pageants and Sports*. London: Routledge, 1882.

Harney, Marion. *Place-Making for the Imagination: Horace Walpole and Strawberry Hill*. Aldershot, UK: Ashgate, 2013.

Harris, Oliver. 'Antiquarian Attitudes: Crossed Legs, Crusaders and the Evolution of an Idea'. *The Antiquaries Journal* 90 (2010), pp. 401–40.

———— 'Beards: True and False'. *Church Monuments* 28 (2013), pp. 124–32.

—————— 'A Crusading "Captain in Khaki": Sir Thomas Brock's Monument to Charles Grant Seely at Gatcombe (Isle of Wight)'. *Church Monuments* 33 (2018), pp. 97–119.

Hayden, Eric S. *A Guide to the Church of St Mary the Virgin Brading, Isle of Wight*, Brading, UK,1982.

Hayward, R.L. *Yesterday in Sullington. The Church, the Parish and the Manor.* Sullington, UK: St. Mary's Church, 1981.

Henderson, George. *Gothic.* Harmondsworth, UK: Penguin, 1967.

Horswell, Mike. *The Rise and Fall of British Crusader Medievalism, c. 1825–1945.* London: Routledge, 2018.

—————— 'Creating Chivalrous Imperial Crusaders: The Crusades in Juvenile Literature from Scott to Newbolt, 1825–1917'. In *Engaging the Crusades: Perceptions of the Crusades in the Nineteenth and Twentieth Centuries.* vol. 1. eds. Mike Horswell and Jonathan Phillips. London: Routledge, 2018, pp. 48–79.

—————— 'From "Superstitious Veneration" to "War to Defend Christendom"': The Crusades in the *Encyclopaedia Britannica* 1771–2018'. In *The Legacy of the Crusades: History and Memory.* eds. Torben K. Nielsen and Kurt V. Jensen. Turnhout, Belgium: Brepols, forthcoming.

—————— 'Saladin and Richard the Lionheart. Entangled Memories'. In *The Making of Crusading Heroes and Villains.* eds. Mike Horswell and Kristen Skottki. London: Routledge, 2020, pp. 75–94.

—————— 'New Crusaders and Crusading Echoes: The Modern Memory and Legacy of the Crusades in the West and Beyond'. In *The Cambridge History of the Crusades.* ed. Jonathan Phillips. Cambridge: CUP, forthcoming.

Hosler, Jon. *The Siege of Acre 1189–1191.* New Haven, CT: Yale University Press, 2018.

Houghton, Walter. ed. *The Wellesley Index to Victorian Periodicals, 1824–1900*, 5 vols. Toronto: University of Toronto Press, 1966–89.

Housley, Norman. *The Later Crusades from Lyons to Alcazar, 1274–1580.* Oxford: OUP, 1992.

Hurlock, Kathryn. 'Cheshire and the Crusades'. *Transactions of the Historical Society of Lancashire and Cheshire* 159 (2010), pp. 1–18.

—————— *Wales and the Crusades, 1095–1291.* Cardiff, UK: University of Wales Press, 2011.

—————— *Britain, Ireland and the Crusades, c. 1000–1300.* Basingstoke, UK: Palgrave Macmillan, 2013.

—————— 'A Transformed Life? Geoffrey of Dutton, the Fifth Crusade and the Holy Cross of Norton'. *Northern History* 54 (2017), pp. 15–27.

—————— *Medieval Welsh Pilgrimage.* Basingstoke, UK: Palgrave Macmillan, 2018.

James, Louis. *Fiction for the Working Man, 1830–50.* Oxford: OUP, 1963.

Johns-Putra, Adeline. 'Eleanor Anne Porden's Coeur de Lion: History, Epic and Romance'. *Women's Writing* 19 (2012), pp. 351–71.

Jones, Brian J. *Washington Irving: An American Original.* New York: Arcade, 2008.

Kaufman, Paul. 'The Reading of Southey and Coleridge: The Record of Their Borrowing from the Bristol Library, 1793–98'. *Modern Philology* 2 (1923–4), pp. 317–20.

Klancher, Jon P. *The Making of the English Reading Audiences 1790–1832.* Madison: University of Wisconsin Press, 1987.

Knobler, Adam. 'Holy Wars, Empires, and the Portability of the Past: The Modern Uses of Medieval Crusades'. *Comparative Studies in Society and History* 48 (2006), pp. 293–325.

Knusel, Christopher J. et al. 'The Identity of the St. Bees Lady, Cumbria. An Oesteobiographical Approach'. *Medieval Archaeology* 54 (2010), pp. 271–311.

Lancaster, Charles. *Seeing England: Antiquaries, Travellers and Naturalists.* Stroud, UK: Nonsuch, 2008.

Larking, L.B. Rev. 'On the Heart Shrine in Leybourne Church'. *Archaeologia Cantiana* 5 (1863), pp. 133–94, and 7 (1868), pp. 323–9.

Lawrence, Jason. *Tasso's Art and Afterlives. Tasso's Gerusalemme Liberata in England.* Manchester, UK: MUP, 2017.

Leask, Nigel. *Stepping Westward.* Oxford: OUP, 2020.

Lees-Milne, James. *Diaries 1942–54: Ancestral Voices and Prophesying Peace.* London: Chatto and Windus, 1975.

Lloyd, Simon D. *English Society and the Crusade, 1216–1307.* Oxford: OUP, 1988.

Loomis, Roger S. 'The Pas Saladin in Art and Heraldry'. In *Studies in Art and Literature for Bella de Costa Greene.* ed. Dorothy Miner. Princeton, NJ: Princeton University Press, 1954, pp. 83–92.

MacCarthy, Fiona. *William Morris: A Life for Our Time.* London: Faber and Faber, 1995.

Mackenzie, John M. 'In Touch with the Infinite: The BBC and the Empire, 1923–53'. In *Imperialism and Popular Culture.* Manchester, UK: MUP, 1986, pp. 165–92.

Maclagan, Michael, 'Genealogy and Heraldry in the Sixteenth and Seventeenth Centuries'. In *English Historical Scholarship in the Sixteenth and Seventeenth Centuries.* ed. Levi Fox. Oxford: OUP, 1956, pp. 31–49.

Macquarrie, Allan. *Scotland and the Crusades, 1095–1560.* Edinburgh: John Donald, 1985.

Malan, Dan, *Gustave Dore. A Comprehensive Biography and Bibliography.* St. Louis, MO: MCE Publishing, 1996.

Manion, Lee. *Narrating the Crusades: Loss and Recovery in Medieval and Early Modern English Literature.* Cambridge: CUP, 2014.

——— 'Renaissance Crusading Literature: Memory, Translation and Adaptation'. In *The Cambridge Companion to the Literature of the Crusades.* ed. Anthony Bale, pp. 232–48. Cambridge: CUP, 2019.

Mason, Emma. 'Legends of the Beauchamps' Ancestors: The Use of Baronial Propaganda in Medieval England'. *Journal of Medieval History* 10 (1984), pp. 25–40.

Mee, Arthur. *Dorset.* London: Hodder & Stoughton, 1939.

Meisel, Martin, *Realizations: Narrative, Pictorial and Theatrical Arts in Nineteenth-Century England.* Princeton, NJ: Princeton University Press, 1983.

Miller, Derek. 'Daniel Deronda and Allegories of Empire'. In *George Eliot and Europe.* ed. John Rignall. Aldershot, UK: Ashgate, 1997.

Muldoon, James. 'Mad Men on Crusade: Religious Madness and the Origins of the First Crusade'. In *Seven Myths of the Crusades.* eds. Alfred J. Andrea and Andrew Holt. Indianapolis, IN: Hackett, 2015, pp. 29–48.

New, Chester W. *The Life of Henry Brougham to 1830.* Oxford: Clarendon Press, 1961.

Nicholas, Alvin. *Supernatural Wales.* Gloucestershire, UK: Amberley, 2013.

Nora, Pierre. *Realms of Memory: Rethinking the French Past.* 3 vols. New York: Columbia University Press, 1996–8.

Orme, Nicholas. 'Cornwall and the Third Crusade'. *Journal of the Royal Institution of Cornwall* (2005), pp. 71–7.

Paul, Nicholas L. *To Follow In Their Footsteps. The Crusades and Family Memory in the High Middle Ages.* London: Cornell University Press, 2012.

——— and Suzanne Yeager. eds. *Remembering the Crusades: Myth, Image and Identity.* Baltimore: John Hopkins University Press, 2012.

Pevsner, Nikolaus and David W. Lloyd. *Buildings of England: Hampshire and the Isle of Wight.* New Haven, CT: Yale, 2006.

——— and Alexandra Wedgwood. *Buildings of England: Warwickshire.* London: Penguin, 1966.

Phillips, Jonathan. *Holy Warriors: A Modern History of the Crusades.* London: Vintage, 2012.

Powell, James. *Anatomy of a Crusade, 1213–21.* Philadelphia: University of Pennsylvania Press, 1986.

Probert, Geoffrey. 'The Riddles of Bures Unravelled'. *Essex Archaeology and History* 126 (1984–5), pp. 53–64.

Pugh, Jane. *Welsh Ghostly Encounters.* Llanwrst, UK: Gwasg Garreg Gwalch, 1990.

Redding, Cyrus. *An Illustrated Itinerary of the County of Lancaster.* London: How and Parsons, 1842.

Rees, Revd. Tony. *Guidebook to St. Mary's Church, Chirk,* 2004.

Reeve, Matthew M. 'The Painted Chamber at Westminster, Edward I and the Crusade'. *Viator* 37 (2006), pp. 189–221.

Richards, Raymond. *Old Cheshire Churches.* London: Batsford, 1947.

Riley-Smith, Jonathan. *The First Crusaders, 1095–1131.* Cambridge: CUP, 1997.

——— *The Crusades, Christianity and Islam.* New York: Columbia University Press, 2008

——— *The Crusades: A History.* 3rd edition. London: Bloomsbury, 2014.

Rothstein, David. 'Forming the Chivalric Subject: Felicia Hemans and the Cultural Uses of History'. *Victorian Literature and Culture* 27 (1999), pp. 49–69.

Sattin, Anthony. *Young Lawrence. A Portrait of the Legend as a Young Man.* London: John Murray, 2014.

Saul, Nigel. *English Church Monuments in the Middle Ages: History and Representation.* Oxford: OUP, 2008.

Saunders, Clare B. 'Louise Stuart Costello and Women's War Poetry'. *The Wordsworth Circle* 43 (2012), pp. 178–82.

Schoch, Richard. *Queen Victoria and the Theatre of Her Age.* Manchester: MUP, 2004.

Scott-Giles, C. Wilfrid. *The Romance of Heraldry.* London: J.M. Dent, 1929.

——— *The Wimsey Family: A Fragmentary History Compiled from Correspondence with Dorothy L. Sayers.* London: Gollancz, 1977.

Shaw, Graham. 'India'. In *The Edinburgh History of the Book: Ambition and Industry, 1800–80.* vol. 3. ed. Bill Bell. Edinburgh: Edinburgh University Press, 2007.

Siedschlag, Beatrice N. *English Participation in the Crusades, 1150–1220.* Menasha, WI: Collegiate Press, 1939.

Siberry, Elizabeth. 'Tasso and the Crusades: History of a Legacy'. *Journal of Medieval History* 19 (1993), pp. 163–9.

——— 'Images of the Crusades in the Nineteenth and Twentieth Centuries'. In *The Oxford Illustrated History of the Crusades.* ed. Jonathan Riley-Smith. Oxford: OUP, 1995.

——— *The New Crusaders: Images of the Crusades in the 19th and Early 20th Centuries.* Aldershot, UK: Ashgate, 2000.

——— 'The Crusader's Departure and Return: A Much Later Perspective'. In *Gendering the Crusades.* eds. Susan Edgington and Sarah Lambert. Cardiff, UK: University of Wales Press, 2001, pp. 177–90.

——— 'Images and Perceptions of the Military Orders in Nineteenth-Century Britain'. *Ordines Militares-Colloquia Torunensia Historica* 11 (2001), 197–210.

——— 'Nineteenth Century Perspectives of the First Crusade' in *The Experience of Crusading: Western Approaches.* vol. 1. eds. Marcus Bull and Norman Housley. Cambridge: CUP, 2003, pp. 281–93.

——— 'A Crickhowell Crusader: The Case of the Missing Hands'. *Brycheiniog* 16 (2013), pp. 101–9.

——— 'The Crusades: The Nineteenth-Century Readers' Perspective'. In *Engaging the Crusades: Perceptions of the Crusades in the Nineteenth and Twentieth Centuries.* Vol. 1. eds. Mike Horswell and Jonathan Phillips. London: Routledge, 2018, pp. 7–27.

——— 'Memorials to Crusaders: The Use of Crusade Imagery in First World War Memorials in Britain'. In *The Legacy of the Crusades.* eds. Kurt Jensen and Torben Nielsen. Turnhout, Belgium: Brepols, forthcoming.

——— 'Saint Louis: A Crusader King and Hero for Victorian and First World War Britain and Ireland'. In *Engaging the Crusades: The Making of Crusading Heroes and Villains.* Vol. 4. eds. Mike Horswell and Kristin Skottki. London: Routledge, 2020, pp. 95–111.

——— 'Variations on a Theme: Harry Pirie-Gordon and the Order of Sanctissima Sophia'. In *Piety, Pugnacity and Property. Military Orders.* Vol. 7. ed. Nicholas Morton. London: Routledge, 2020, pp. 237–47.

Simpson, Murray. 'Private Libraries'. In *The Edinburgh History of the Book in Scotland, 1707–1800*. eds. Stephen W. Brown and Warren McDougall. Edinburgh: Edinburgh University Press, 2012, pp. 313–26.

Skottki, Kristin. 'The Dead, the Revived and the Recreated Pasts: "Structural Amnesia" in Representations of Crusade History'. In *Perceptions of the Crusades from the Nineteenth to the Twenty-First Centuries*. eds. Mike Horswell and Jonathan Phillips, London: Routledge, 2018, pp. 107–33.

Speck, William, A. *Robert Southey: Entire Man of Letters*. New Haven, CT: Yale University Press, 2006.

Stevenson, Lionel. *The Pre-Raphaelite Poets*. Chapel Hill: University of North Carolina Press, 1972.

Sullivan, Alvin. ed. *British Literary Magazines: The Victorian and Edwardian Age 1837–1913*. London: Greenwood Press, 1985.

Sweet, Rosemary. *Antiquaries: The Discovery of the Past in Eighteenth-Century Britain*. London: A. and C. Black, 2004.

Swenson, Astrid. 'Crusader Heritages and Imperial Preservation'. *Past and Present* 226 (2015), pp. 27–56.

Thomas, Lowell. *With Lawrence in Arabia*. London: Hutchinson, 1924.

Thomas, Mark. *A History of Brougham Hall and High Head Castle*. Chichester, UK: Phillimore, 1992.

Treuherz, Julian. *Victorian Painting*. London: Thames and Hudson, 1993.

Treves, Frederick. *Highways and Byways in Dorset*. London: Macmillan, 1934.

Turner, Margaret N. *Joseph Murray Ince 1806–59: The Painter of Presteigne*. Almeley, UK: Logaston Press, 2006.

Tyerman, Christopher. *England and the Crusades, 1095–1588*. Chicago: Chicago University Press, 1988.

———— *The Invention of the Crusades*. New York: Palgrave Macmillan, 1998.

———— *The Debate on the Crusades*. Manchester: MUP, 2011.

Vale, Juliet. *Edward III and Chivalry: Chivalric Society and its Context 1270–1350*. Woodbridge, UK: Boydell, 1982.

Vincent, Nicholas. *The Lucys of Charlecote: The Invention of a Warwickshire Family, 1170–1302*. Stratford-upon-Avon, UK: Dugdale Society, 2002.

Wagner, Anthony. 'Heraldry'. In *Medieval England*. ed. Austin L. Poole. Oxford: OUP, 1958, pp. 338–81.

———— *Heralds of England. A History of the Office and College of Arms*. London: Her Majesty's Stationery Office, 1967.

Wainwright, Clive. *The Romantic Interior: The British Collector at Home, 1750–80*. New Haven, CT: Yale University Press, 1989.

Waller, John G. 'The Lords of Cobham, Their Monuments and Their Church'. *Archaeologia Cantiana* 11 (1877), pp. 49–112.

Weisert, John J. 'Graf von Gleichen "Redivivus"'. *Monatshefte* 40 (1948), pp. 465–70.

Whatley, Laura J., 'Romance, Crusade and the Orient in King Henry III's Royal Chambers'. *Viator* 44 (2013), pp. 175–99.

Whitla, William. 'William Morris's "The Mosque Rising in the Place of the Temple of Solomon": A Critical text'. *Pre-Raphaelite Studies* 9 (2000), pp. 43–81.

Williams, Stanley T. *The Life of Washington Irving.* Oxford: OUP, 1935.

Williams, Stephen. 'Some Monumental Effigies in Wales'. *Archaeologia Cambrensis* 11 (1877), pp. 49–112.

Williamson, Gillian. *English Masculinity in the Gentleman's Magazine, 1731–1815.* Basingstoke, UK: Palgrave Macmillan, 2016.

Woodcock, Thomas and John M. Robinson. *Heraldry in Historic Houses.* London: National Trust, 1999.

Wright, Angela. *Britain, France and the Gothic, 1764–1820.* Cambridge: CUP, 2013.

Wyatt, Matthew D. and John B. Waring. *The Byzantine and Romanesque Court in the Crystal Palace.* London: Bradbury and Evans, 1954.

Yorke-Long, Alan. 'George II and Handel'. *History Today* (1951), pp. 33–9.

Index

Printed in the United States
by Baker & Taylor Publisher Services